KEYS TO STARTING A SMALL BUSINESS

Joel G. Siegel, Ph.D., CPA
Self-Employed Accounting Practitioner
Professor of Accounting and Finance
Queens College of the City University of New York

Jae K. Shim, Ph.D.
Financial and Managerial Consultant
Professor of Business
California State University, Long Beach

BARRON'S

All inquiries should be addressed to:
Barron's Educational Series, Inc.
250 Wireless Boulevard
Hauppauge, New York 11788

Library of Congress Catalog Card Number 90-49826

International Standard Book No. 0-8120-4487-8

Library of Congress Cataloging in Publication Data
Siegel, Joel G.
    Keys to starting a small business / Joel G. Siegel, Jae K.
Shim.
        p.   cm.
    Includes index.
    ISBN 0-8120-4487-8
    1. New business enterprises.   2. Small business.   I. Shim,
Jae K.   II. Title.
HD62.5.S5565   1991
658.1'141—dc20   90-49826
                                                                        CIP

PRINTED IN THE UNITED STATES OF AMERICA
56789   5500   9876

CONTENTS

Section V—Accounting

Section VI—Taxes

Section VII—Marketing

Section VIII—Operations

Section IX—Personnel

Section X—Types of Businesses

INTRODUCTION

An entrepreneur is one who manages, organizes, and assumes the risk of a business. The entrepreneur starts a business because of a plan or idea that he or she believes will work.

The Small Business Administration defines a small business as one that is independently owned, is locally operated, is not dominant in its field of operation, grosses less than $3 million annually, and has fewer than 100 employees.

More than 30 percent of American businesses are considered small. Many of today's giant companies, such as Woolworth and J C Penney, began as small businesses.

Before starting a new business, ask some tough questions, including: Who are the competition and can I beat them? What are the downside risks? What is the trend in the industry? How does the economy look? Can I raise the funds? Why is my product or service better than the competition's? Do I really know how to run a successful business?

At the very beginning, get competent professional advice from an attorney and an accountant. You want to know from them what to do and what not to do. An attorney will know how to form the business legally and how to protect you from possible lawsuits. An accountant is needed to handle recordkeeping and tax matters. You must have an accountant to set up the books so you will know how your financial position looks. You may have to take corrective financial steps to "stay on course."

Depending on whose statistics you follow, between 50 and 90 percent of new businesses fail within the first couple of years. Why? There are a number of different possibilities, including lack of adequate capital, failure to keep track of the money, deficient recordkeeping, poor internal control, inadequate understanding of the competition, mismanagement of business affairs, poor organization, and lack of knowledge of the features and prices of the products and/or services offered.

With regard to inadequate handling of money, you must know where the cash inflow is coming from and how dependable it is. Is revenue stable? What are the sources of capital? How difficult will it be to raise additional funds? You have to know in advance what the expenses will be, when these expenses must be met, and whether the expenses are reasonable. You must make allowances for unexpected contingencies, or you may find yourself short of cash. You must constantly do your homework when it comes to finances!

1

DETERMINING HOW MUCH TO PAY FOR THE BUSINESS

In determining the value of a prospective business, consider the type of business and its major activities, industry conditions, competition, marketing requirements, management possibilities, risk factors, earning potential, and financial health of the business.

The most common valuation approaches are based on earnings or assets. Under the earnings approach, adjusted average net income may be capitalized at an appropriate multiple; with the assets approach, assets are valued at fair (i.e., appraised) market value. Values of comparable companies in the industry may also provide useful norms. A source of comparative industry information for small businesses is *Financial Studies of the Small Business* (Washington, D.C.: Financial Research Associates, 1984).

Valuation Based on Earnings. Net income should be multiplied by an appropriate multiplier to approximate the company's value. The multiplier should be higher for a low-risk business and lower for a high-risk one. For example, the multiplier for a high-risk business may be 1 while that for a low-risk business may be 3. A five-year average adjusted historical earnings figure is typically representative. The five years' experienced earnings record up to the valuation date reflects the company's earning power. The computation follows:

Average Adjusted Earnings (5 years)
× Multiplier (based on industry norm) = Valuation

Weighted-average adjusted historical earnings, in which more weight is given to the most recent years, are more representative than a simple average. This makes sense because current earnings reflect current prices and recent business activity. In the case of a five-year weighted average, the current year is assigned a weight of 5 while the initial year is assigned a weight of 1. The multiplier is then applied to the weighted-average five-year adjusted historical earnings to derive a valuation. An example follows:

Year	Net Income	×	Weight	=	Total
1990	$130,000	×	5	=	$ 650,000
1989	120,000	×	4	=	480,000
1988	100,000	×	3	=	300,000
1987	80,000	×	2	=	160,000
1986	90,000	×	1	=	90,000
			15		$1,680,000

Weighted-Average 5-year earnings:
    $1,680,000/15 = $112,000

Weighted-average 5-year earnings	$112,000
× Multiple	× 3*
Capitalization-of-Earnings Valuation	$336,000

Present Value of Future Cash Flows. A company may be valued at the present value of future cash earnings and the present value of the expected selling price. The growth rate in cash earnings may be based on prior growth, future expectations and the inflation rate. The discount rate may be based on the market interest rate of a low risk asset investment. Cash earnings are important because they represent profits backed up by cash that can be used for investment purposes. Refer to present value tables in an accounting or financial text.

Valuation Based on Book Value (Net Worth). The business may be valued at the book value of the net assets at the most *current* balance sheet date.

*The multiple may be based on such factors as earnings stability, risk, anticipated growth, or liquidity.

Fair Market Value of Net Assets. The fair market value of the net tangible assets of the company may be based on independent appraisal. An addition is made for goodwill. A business broker, who handles the purchase and sale of businesses, may be hired to appraise the tangible property. Usually, the fair market value of the assets exceeds their book value.

Gross Revenue Multiplier. A business value may be computed by multiplying the sales by a revenue multiplier typical in the industry. The industry norm gross revenue multiplier is based on the average ratio of market price to sales. For example, if revenue is $5 million and the multiplier is .1, the valuation is: $5,000,000 × .1 = $500,000. If reported earnings are suspect, this method may be advisable.

Values of Similar Businesses. The market price of a comparable company in the industry should be obtained. What did similar businesses sell for recently? What would be the price for this particular concern? Although an identical match is not possible, reasonable comparability between companies should exist (e.g., size, product, structure, diversity). Industry sources include Dun and Bradstreet.

Integration of Methods. The valuation of the company may be estimated based on a weighted-average value of several methods. The most weight should typically be placed on the earnings methods and the least on the assets approaches. For example, assume that the fair market value of the net assets method provides a value of $3 million and the earnings method gives a value of $2.4 million. If the earnings method is assigned a weight of 2 and the fair market value of net assets method is assigned a weight of 1, the business valuation is:

Method	Amount	×	Weight	=	Total
Fair Market Value of Net Assets	$3,000,000	×	1	=	$3,000,000
Capitalization-of-Excess Earnings	$2,400,000	×	2	=	$4,800,000
			3	=	$7,800,000
					÷ 3
Valuation					$2,600,000

2

WHERE SHOULD THE NEW BUSINESS BE LOCATED?

The best location varies with the type of business. It is usually best for a retail store to be near other retail stores, preferably in a shopping area. For example, a supermarket generates a lot of traffic; proximity to one may increase your traffic flow. A mail order business should be near a post office. A distributor should be as close as possible to customers, provided rent is low. Choice of location for a manufacturer depends on the product line and marketing factors.

Generally, a retail business should be near its potential customers. Population data may be obtained from a town office or the Small Business Administration. Determine the buying patterns of the population: Is it consistent with your proposed product or service? Is the customer profile in conformity with your product (e.g., age, occupation, sex)? An economically healthy community is usually best.

Clothing stores and jewelry stores are usually more successful in main or outlying central shopping areas. Grocery stores, drugstores, gasoline stations, and bakeries do well on major thoroughfares and on neighborhood streets outside of the main shopping districts.

The store should be visible if you rely on impulse buying. A corner location at a busy intersection is preferred because of constant pedestrian flow. If people need cars to reach your store, you will need ample parking.

Service companies not relying on impulse buying (e.g., beauty parlors, travel agencies) need less visibility but more attractive decor, internal comfort, and accessibility.

The exterior and interior design of the store should project the personality of the business.

In looking at a location in a shopping center, determine what competing stores exist. Also, look at traffic patterns. What stores are about to open? What are the rentals? Will your business do well in lively surroundings in an active mall (e.g., record shop, bookstore, ice cream parlor)?

If your business is more vulnerable to pilferage, remember that activity is more likely to happen in a shopping mall. Stores such as a conservative, high-priced men's store may do less well in a mall.

Be cautious in signing a lease in a shopping mall that has not yet opened. If the contractor cannot sign enough tenants, he or she may go out of business. Make sure your agreement spells out your exact location and its specifications. Try to get a "no-compete" clause prohibiting the opening of a store that would be in direct competition with yours (e.g., only one pet store). What other types of businesses will be opening, and how will they affect your business?

The location of your business should preferably be in a low-crime area.

A wholesale business should be located so as to minimize transportation costs. The warehouse should be centrally located to reduce delivery costs to regular customers. There should be easy access to major highways for quick travel.

In deciding on a location for a small plant, you should seek a place near your market, customers, suppliers, raw material sources, and skilled labor. An industrial park may be suitable. Would the neighborhood population be receptive to your business? Can you obtain tax incentives from the local government?

3

SHOULD YOU BUY AN ALREADY EXISTING BUSINESS?

In deciding if it pays to purchase an already established business, there are many things to consider. The first thing you should do is visit the business and observe such aspects as location, appearance, and clientele. You should request background information about the business, including a list of customers and financial statements. Why is the owner *really* selling? Is there anything wrong? If so, what is it? The reason given for selling the business may not be the actual reason, so you will have to be a detective. Is revenue down? If so, why? Is there increased competition? If so, from whom? Is the neighborhood changing? If so, how? Have there been product liability or other lawsuit problems?

Do your homework by speaking with other business-people in the area, customers, suppliers, current and former employees, and trade association staff. Ask for bank references, and contact the Better Business Bureau for previous complaints. Also, obtain a report on the company from Dun and Bradstreet. The last thing you need is a lemon.

What has been the historical background of this business? Has there been a previous bankruptcy? Has the owner failed to make timely payments?

You will want to learn about the following:

1. *Sales and Net Income.* Project future revenue and earnings. Prior and current years' figures may serve as a benchmark. Ask for copies of the fi-

nancial statements and tax returns. Prepare relevant ratios, such as the profit margin (net income/sales). Make sure to retain a certified public accountant (CPA) to review and audit the records for correctness. For example, are expense/sales ratios in line with expectations? If the potential seller refuses to provide important records, a red light should go on in your mind.

NOTE: The further into the future you project financial figures, the less reliable they are because of economic uncertainties. Typically, do not forecast more than five years ahead.

What can you do to improve the financial condition of the business?

Besides retaining a CPA, seek the professional advice of an attorney, an insurance agent, and a banker.

2. *Accounts Receivable.* Age the accounts receivable for possible uncollectibility. Is the customer base concentrated or diversified? Is the credit policy too liberal or stringent? Which customers are likely to stay with you if you buy the business?

3. *Inventory.* Observe the inventory, and have it appraised. What is its condition and salability? Can you get the going rate for the merchandise?

4. *Goodwill.* Does the business have a good name? Will the seller's leaving have an adverse effect, and if so, to what degree?

5. *Proprietary Items.* Are proprietary items (e.g., patents) worth anything? If so, can you keep them?

6. *Building, Equipment, and Furniture.* What is the condition and age of the capital assets? What are they worth? What would the cost be to replace old assets? Do you have to modify the equipment to make it suitable for your own use?

7. *Liabilities.* Are there any liabilities, such as unpaid bills, pending litigation, or back taxes, that have been incurred by the prior business owner and for which you will be responsible? If so, how

much are they? Seek the advice of a CPA and an attorney. Your purchasing contract should stipulate that any claims against the business before you took ownership are the responsibility of the seller.

8. *Budget.* Prepare a budget of future sales, expenses, and profits.

9. *Cost Control.* Are current costs "fat"? Can you cut costs to reduce areas of inefficiency?

10. *Contracts.* Are there favorable contracts (e.g., low rental leases, low interest mortgages) that may be transferred to you? How long do the contracts have to go? What are the renewal terms?

11. *Suppliers.* Will suppliers accommodate you when you take over? Are suppliers reliable, or is a change needed?

12. *Quality Control.* Can you improve on the quality of the product?

13. *Product and/or Service Market.* Is the market for the product and/or service expanding, stable, or declining?

14. *Legal Requirements.* Will you as the new owner be required to obtain certain permits and licenses? If so, what kind? An attorney should be consulted.

15. *Customer Lists.* If it is a mail order business, will you own the customer mailing list?

16. *Major Personnel.* Will key personnel remain after you buy the business?

17. *Production Efficiencies.* Can you correct current production inefficiencies and reduce manufacturing costs, perhaps by buying up-to-date equipment?

18. *Franchises.* Do you have the exclusive franchise in the area, and what are the contractual terms?

19. *Unique Situation.* Perhaps the prospective seller has done well because of unique reasons (e.g., race, religion). If you do not have this same background, you may run into problems.

20. *Seller Cooperation.* Will the seller provide consultation for a reasonable period of time when you take over? Will the seller introduce you to major customers? Have the seller sign a noncompeting agreement so customers may not move to him or her after the sale.

4

THE BUSINESS PLAN

Before starting a business, learn about it. You should be familiar with the industry's profit percentages, sales volume, pricing, and suppliers and with problems faced by other companies. This information can be obtained from several sources, such as trade magazines, professional associations, manufacturers, and the Small Business Administration. The latter will help you start your business by providing free information and counseling.

A business plan is a must when you start a business. The business plan is a road map to guide you through the precarious first few years. It serves as a written guide for your future operations and covers your short- and long-term goals, details about your business, your management strategy, your method of operation, and timetables. Of course, the goals must be realistic.

The business plan may take all aspects of the business into consideration, including manufacturing of the products, and the financing and marketing of those products. It enables you to see your limitations and helps you to avoid unexpected problems. It also allows you to plan for alternative courses of action in specific situations. You should keep records indicating what goals have been met and what progress has been made toward reaching other goals.

The business plan summarizes financial facts and figures, and projects future income and profits. The plan is a valuable analytical tool for guiding your operations and serves as a means to attract lenders or investors. It shows how much needs to be financed, how and where the money will be spent, how a return will be generated, and how money will be repaid. The plan also provides an analysis of the market, competition, product, and production. The business plan must stand up to critical evaluation and scrutiny by investors and creditors. The plan should be comprehensible and professionally presented. Investors and creditors feel more confident when their money is placed in a professionally managed business.

You have to develop a course of action. For example, you should decide what marketing strategy (methods for selling your product or service) to use for your business.

In the business plan, answer the following questions: When will the company show a profit, who will work, and how many hours will be required? You should also schedule the purchase of certain equipment and supplies. If you are starting a business that has seasonal peaks and valleys, be sure to allow for the busy and slow months. How and when do you see the company growing? What must you do to achieve growth?

The business plan should consist of three main parts: a brief statement of purpose, the main body of the plan, and the supporting documents.

The Cover Sheet. This includes the name of business, name of principal, address and phone number of business.

Statement of Purpose. Description of business, product or service, market, competition, location, management, personnel, application and expected effect of loan (if any), and summary.

Body of Plan. Sources and uses of funds, capital equipment list, pro forma balance sheet, break-even analysis, income projections (including three-year summary, detail by month for first year, and detail by quarter for second and third years), pro forma cash flow (including detail by month for first year, detail by quarter for second and third years), and deviation analysis.

Supporting Documents. Personal resumes of owners; personal financial requirements and statements; budgets; letters of reference; copies of leases, contracts, or legal documents; anything else of relevance to the plan.

How can you present your case in a manner that will convince the loan officer and overcome any business prejudices? This can be done through a loan proposal. A loan proposal is an up-to-date business plan that shows how the bank's loan will improve your company's worth. Normally, the loan proposal begins with an overview of your company's history, the amount of money you need, the proposed use and allocation of the loan proceeds, and the collateral you have available to secure the loan.

The loan proposal should include:

- A cover letter stating the amount requested for your proposed term and a brief survey of your business and its financial goals.
- A market analysis explaining how your concept fits in with current business trends and why it will succeed in the marketplace.
- A description of how the business will be run. Include resumes of key personnel.
- A financial plan including current and projected figures. Loan officers are particularly interested in liquidity and profitability.

5

FINANCING THE SMALL BUSINESS

Probably the largest obstacle facing entrepreneurs is the need for startup financing to open for business. The search for funding provides a sobering glimpse of reality. The entrepreneur needs initial monies for licenses and fees, remodeling, furniture and equipment, professional fees (e.g., attorney fees), inventory, supplies, rent, wages, advertising, and other costs associated with opening the doors. After you do start up, you will then incur day-to-day operating expenses, which may be a financial hardship until you start to become profitable. In financing the business, remember that most businesses lose money in the first and second years of operation. Later, you will need growth financing to expand and reach the greatest possible potential.

Before seeking financing, do your homework. How much money do you need and why? Itemize all your expected costs. What will you be doing with the money? Be prepared to give realistic financial projections. The actual funds you have to invest from all sources must be sufficient to meet these costs in order to succeed with your venture.

If you display confidence in the business, you will transmit your feeling to potential creditors and investors. Ask for a bit more money than you think you will need, since there will undoubtedly be some unforeseen expenses to be covered.

In deciding upon a source of financing, consider the following:

- *Availability*. What sources may you realistically tap?
- *Cost*. What is the cost (e.g., interest rate) associated with the financing source? Will you be able to meet

13

such costs when due or will they generate cash problems?

- *Flexibility*. Are there any lender restrictions that may inhibit your freedom of action or ability to obtain further financing? Are there any limitations on how you can use the funds?
- *Control*. Will you be giving up any control in the company in obtaining the financing?
- *Risk*. What is the risk associated with the particular funding source? Will you have to make early, significant loan payments?

The ability to finance a business depends on its reputation and prospects, the amount of money needed to start and operate the business, and the owner's personal resources. If you are well known in your field, you may be able to finance with a substantial amount of outside capital. But if you are starting without these advantages, you may have to depend more on your personal resources. Some people have started businesses successfully using their personal savings, or borrowing against their houses or other assets. The advantage of using your *own* funds as much as possible is that you do not have to go through the time-consuming process and hassle of obtaining outside funding. Also, you do not have to worry about repaying the loan or giving up an equity ownership interest. However, few businesses can operate long on personal financing. Further, it is probably not advisable to place all of your personal resources into a business because of the risk of losing your investment.

One source of funds is relatives and friends. This is an attractive source because it is quick, less costly, and easy. There are fewer written reports and statements to prepare as well as less legal work and fewer disputes between the parties. It is best to treat this money as a loan rather than an equity interest; in this way, you can keep total control and achieve the maximum reward for your services. Also, if you give an equity interest, others may interfere in the smooth running and decision-making processes of the business.

You can borrow against the cash surrender value of

14

your life insurance policy. For example, you may decide to borrow up to 80 percent of the amount accumulated in the policy. You then will pay interest on the loan in addition to the premium.

An often overlooked source of money is your suppliers. Trade creditors and equipment manufacturers are involved in the operation and have an interest in seeing it succeed. They understand your business, are connected with it, and therefore may prove to be sympathetic lenders.

Equity and debt financing are discussed in Keys 6 and 8. To obtain such financing, you will probably have to prepare a proposal.

The financing proposal should highlight the nature and objectives of the business, financial health, the owner's background, references, product line and/or services, markets to be served, customer base, competition, suppliers, manufacturing costs, cost structure, proposed financing terms, dollar financing required, proposed use of the money, and description of personnel. The proposal should include how much you need, the preferred terms, and repayment preferences. Projected and actual financial statements, including a balance sheet, income statement, and statement of cash flows, will also be needed. Cash flow projections for the next year are crucial. By projecting what you think you are going to sell and spend during the upcoming months, you can see any potential financial difficulties on the horizon.

Finders may be used to obtain a loan or equity capital. They charge a percentage commission based on the financing raised. The fees vary considerably, ranging from 1 percent to 20 percent. Finders are listed in advertisements in financial papers (e.g., *The Wall Street Journal*).

6

DEBT FINANCING

When financing assets of a business, you should use the hedging approach. This means that you should finance assets with debt of a similar maturity so that proceeds from the assets are sufficient to pay off the debt when it comes due. For example, it is inadvisable to finance a long-term asset with a short-term debt; the loan will come due before the asset has generated enough cash flow to cover it.

Debt financing may be a simple way to raise money. Basically, it describes any kind of loan. However, lenders can be brutally negative about the prospect of survival of a new business. As reported in the June 1990 issue of *Ideas and Trends,* a newsletter for CPAs, small businesses have been particularly hit by the tightening money market. The newsletter states that small businesses often pay three to five points more in interest rates, are required to put up greater collateral, and need to show a ratio of assets to debt of no less than four to one (double what was required in 1989) to obtain financing.

There are many sources of debt financing, including commercial banks, savings and loan associations, credit unions, commercial credit and sales finance companies, small business investment companies, suppliers, insurance companies, and community development companies. Most lenders will require some form of collateral to guarantee their loans. Such collateral may include real estate, stocks, bonds, cars, cash value of life insurance, inventory, and equipment.

Trade creditors are a good source of financing because funding, essentially a method of buying materials, merchandise, or equipment on credit, is readily available. In effect, it is a cost-free source of financing. Suppliers are

16

often sympathetic because you are a source of business. If you are short of funds, you may want to delay payments to suppliers. However, be careful not to stretch them too far because that may damage your credit rating. When discounts are offered, such as 2/10, net/30, take them if possible because of the high opportunity cost associated with forgoing the discount.

You may also use your *personal credit cards*. You may be able to charge up to several thousand dollars to buy items or services for your business. However, two drawbacks are that the interest rate on credit cards is very high and that you must make minimum monthly payments.

Short-term *bank loans* tend to be granted without too much concern for collateral, since these loans are usually a self-liquidating form of sales made in the ordinary course of business. Medium-term loans, running for one to five years, are more likely to require collateral. These loans are often made to finance machinery and equipment, including furniture and fixtures, and store alteration. A medium-term loan, in contrast to a short-term loan, may impose operating restrictions (e.g., working capital level, further debt financing). Long-term loans run for more than five years. These loans are the least often sought and probably the hardest to get. They are usually linked to specific business purposes, the most common of which include purchase of real property and major expansion. They are backed by specific assets of the business. Obtaining a long-term loan involves a fair amount of paperwork and delay.

Banks are conservative about lending to new businesses. They want a borrower with a reputation and a business that has profit potential. Generally, a bank will not lend money to a new business for the purpose of paying off its debts to other creditors. The bank wants the funds to be used constructively. The bank generally wants the owner to put up a sizable amount of his or her own money to show the owner is confident and is willing to take risk. A good working relationship with bank loan officers will facilitate later financing.

There are various types of bank loans, including:

- *Borrowing against a savings account.* This involves a lower cost, and your deposit still earns interest.
- *Unsecured loan.* To obtain an unsecured loan, you need an excellent credit rating. However, the interest rate may be higher, since there is no collateral.
- *Secured loan.* The loan is backed up by collateral.
- *Term loan.* This is a loan that involves repayment in periodic installments that include principal and interest. A high credit rating and collateral are typically required.
- *Straight loan.* This is a short-term loan payable in a single payment.
- *Line of credit.* The bank agrees to make money available if you need it up to a specified predetermined maximum. It is good for a seasonal business.
- *Cosigner loan.* If your credit rating is a problem, you will need someone of good financial standing to cosign the loan.
- *Real estate loan.* You can take out a mortgage against the value of real estate, including a home equity loan. Typically, you can receive financing for up to 80 percent of the value of the property. A mortgage is a long-term financing source that runs for about 15 to 25 years. Thus, you can delay full payment until far off into the future, minimizing near-term cash squeezes.
- *Equipment loan.* You can get a loan against the value of equipment, typically up to 80 percent of its value. The loan is usually tied to the life of the equipment.
- *Accounts receivable financing.* The bank will advance you money against accounts receivable balances, which serve as security for the loan. Typically, the advance is up to 80 percent of the value of the receivables. When customers remit payments to you, you in turn send the payments to the bank to reduce the loan balance.
- *Inventory financing.* Inventory may be used as collateral for a loan. Typically, the bank will lend you up to 50 percent of the value of the inventory.
- *Warehouse loan.* This is a loan based on warehouse receipts delivered directly by the lender. The lender

has legal possession of the goods while the loan is in effect.

You can sell your accounts receivable to a *factor* to obtain funds. Typically, the factor will advance up to 80 percent of the value of the accounts receivable. Factoring is without recourse, meaning that if the customer does not pay the factor, you are not responsible. Thus, the factor is taking the risk of noncollection. The factor charges a fee on the accounts receivable financed (e.g., 2 percent) and interest on the advanced funds. A factoring arrangement is more costly than other private loans from banks and finance companies.

One attractive alternative for small businesses that are short of cash is *leasing,* since it does not require a capital outlay. Leasing is generally more expensive than borrowing funds from other debt-financing sources.

Many large companies, labor unions, and trade organizations have a *credit union.* They are established to assist employees with loans as well as savings. Some individuals who go into business on a part-time basis finance their small business with a loan from their credit union.

Commercial finance companies provide loans for working capital and inventory financing to small businesses. Typically, the borrower goes to a finance company when he or she is unable to obtain a loan at a bank. Because of the borrower's greater risk, the interest rate on a finance company loan is higher than that of a bank loan. In addition, collateral is usually required.

Community development companies are established by local communities to attract businesses. The most popular type is one that develops shopping malls or industrial parks.

There are many *state business and industrial development corporations* (SBIDCs), supported by state funds, that lend money to small businesses, typically up to 20 years for capital facilities. Each state has its own policy with regard to the degree of risk it will accept and the financing terms. You may contact the chamber of commerce or the business development office.

Venture capitalists may lend funds for a short period of time, usually five years. You may want to obtain a copy of the U.S. Small Business Administration's pamphlet, *A Venture Capital Primer for Small Business*.

Sometimes you can combine debt and equity financing. Called a *convertible debenture,* this instrument begins as a loan and is later converted to a share of the ownership of your business.

When the cost of debt financing is prohibitive, you may opt for equity capital.

7

SMALL BUSINESS ADMINISTRATION

You should contact your local Small Business Administration (SBA) office to determine if you qualify as a small business. Size standards have been established and are subject to change. For example, a retail small business is defined as one in which annual sales or receipts do not exceed $3.5 million to $13.5 million, depending upon the size of the industry.

Before you can apply for an SBA loan, you have to apply first to private sources (e.g., a bank) and be refused a loan on reasonable terms. To obtain an SBA loan, you may have to put up collateral, such as property, plant and equipment, or other suitable assets. A loan application can be obtained from your local SBA office. Also, the SBA provides financial counseling and assistance services.

The two types of SBA loans are business loans and economic opportunity loans. The first type of business loan is one made by a private lender (e.g., a bank) and guaranteed by the SBA. However, there is a ceiling of $500,000 on the SBA's guarantee. The longest maturity available for a regular business loan is 25 years. The second type of business loan is made directly by the SBA. Typically, the interest rate on this loan is slightly lower than the going market interest rate in the money market. This loan is given only when a small business cannot obtain private financing or an SBA guaranteed participating loan with a private lender. There is a maximum of $150,000 if a loan is made directly by the SBA.

Economic opportunity loans are restricted to those of low income or who qualify as disadvantaged. Typically, a $100,000 maximum is placed on such a loan. For this category, the maximum term for a business loan is 15 years and for a working capital loan, 10 years. Collateral is also required.

Small business investment companies (SBICs) and minority enterprise small business investment companies (MESBICs) are both regulated and sponsored by SBA. SBICs look for businesses that have proprietary products and/or products that exhibit a high growth potential. They prefer to loan money to young, aggressive companies that present low risk. The major difference between the SBIC and the MESBIC is that the MESBIC must invest only in minority-owned and managed firms. Both make equity investments and long-term loans, mostly with a five- to seven-year term.

8

EQUITY FINANCING

Another way to raise money for your small business is to issue stock. In effect, you are selling part of the business to someone else. Stock does not have to be repaid, nor is an interest payment required. A stock issuance improves the credit rating of the company relative to issuing debt. However, you are giving up a share of ownership in your business and allowing others to participate in the company's earnings. You may pay dividends to stockholders. Stockholders have limited liability in that they are not personally liable for the debts of the company.

There are several drawbacks to issuing stock. You may be giving up some voting control; ownership interest is diluted; dividends are not tax-deductible; earnings and dividends are spread over more shares outstanding; and the cost of issuing stock is higher than that of debt.

If you decide to issue stock, you should keep adequate shares to compensate for your input in starting the business. In other words, you should receive a quantity of "low-cost" shares commensurate with the services you provided. The remaining shares may be bought by others at the going rate.

A company may issue different classes of common stock. Class A is stock issued to the public and usually has no dividends specified. However, it does usually have voting rights. Class B stock is usually kept by the company's organizers. Dividends are typically not paid on Class B stock until the company has generated sufficient earnings.

Venture capital is typically provided for new, risky businesses without a proven track record but with growth potential. Because of the high risk, venture capitalists will look very closely at your business, including product line, services to be performed, and market potential. Venture capitalists want to know how much money is wanted and for what purpose; they want to know your financial prospects. Typically, they require an equity ownership in your business; often more than a 50 percent ownership interest will be demanded. Although they have a controlling equity interest, venture capitalists will typically let you control the daily activities.

Venture capitalists expect to receive a very high return for the significant risk they are undertaking. For example, they may expect to double their investment in two years. Typically, about $2 million is the maximum available in venture capital funds for a business.

Assistance in finding venture capital private investors may be obtained from Venture Capital Networks, P.O. Box 882, Durham, New Hampshire 03824. A list of venture capital companies may be found in *The Guide to Venture Capital Sources* (Illinois: Capital Publishing Corporation, 10 South LaSalle Street, Chicago, Illinois 60603).

9

SHOULD YOU LEASE RATHER THAN BUY?

A lease is a long-term rental of real or personal property by the lessee. You make periodic rental payments over the life of the lease to the lessor. Information may be obtained from the American Association of Equipment Lessors, 5635 Douglas Avenue, Milwaukee, Wisconsin 53218.

Since leasing does not require an immediate cash outlay, many small businesses choose to lease rather than buy office equipment, machinery, automobiles, and computers. This frees the funds for other purposes. However, the total cost of leasing exceeds that of buying over the long term.

A lease contract contains the following provisions: lease term, renewal option, rental rate, cancellation provision, value of leased item, location where leased item may be used, and who is responsible for maintenance and insurance.

Leasing has several advantages, including the following:

- Payments are spread over a longer time period. The lessor may agree to a flexible payment schedule to coincide with the seasonal nature of the lessee.
- Typically, a purchase option exists, permitting the lessee to obtain the property at a bargain price at the expiration of the lease. This provides the lessee with the flexibility to make the purchase decision based on the value of the property at the termination date.
- The lessor's expert service is made available.
- There are generally fewer financing restrictions placed on the lessee by the lessor than are imposed when obtaining a loan to buy the asset.

25

The obligation for future rental payment may not have to be reported on the balance sheet.
- In bankruptcy or reorganization, the maximum claim of lessors against the business is three years of lease payments. In the case of debt, creditors have a claim for the total amount of the unpaid financing.
- The lessee may avoid having the obsolescence risk of the property if the lessor, in determining the lease payments, fails to estimate accurately the obsolescence of the asset.

However, there are several drawbacks to leasing, including the following:
- The interest cost associated with leasing is typically higher than the interest cost on debt.
- If the property reverts to the lessor at the termination of the lease, the lessee must either sign a new lease or buy the property at higher current prices. Also, the salvage value of the property is realized by the lessor.
- The lessee may have to retain property no longer needed (i.e., obsolete equipment).
- The lessee cannot make improvements to the leased property without the permission of the lessor.

In deciding upon which lessor to use, consider the rental fee and the reliability of the lessor. The lease rate per year is usually lower if you choose a longer rental period. Before using a particular lessor, check references.

Present value analysis may be used to decide whether it is cheaper to buy or lease. Future cash flows are discounted with the use of present value tables and the cheaper alternative is selected.

10

WORKING CAPITAL

Working capital equals current assets less current liabilities. For example, if your current assets are $250,000 and your current liabilities are $100,000, your working capital is $150,000. If working capital is inadequate, you may fail because the business has insufficient funds to meet short-term obligations. Identify the reasons for any material change in working capital.

The major components of working capital are:

- *Cash and Marketable Securities*. These are the most liquid of the current assets.
- *Accounts Receivable*. These represent balances due you from customers. What is the age of accounts receivable? Is there a reasonable relationship between accounts receivable and sales? Search out ways to accelerate cash collections, perhaps by offering a discount for early collection. Risky customers should be avoided because of the possibility of uncollectibility.
- *Inventory*. Inventory represents merchandise held for resale. Watch out for inventory buildups—these may mean problems in selling goods. Is inventory obsolete or perishable? Determine inventory turnover rates by comparing sales to average inventory. However, inadequate stocking may lead to lost business.
- *Accounts Payable*. These are amounts you owe trade creditors on account. Accounts payable is a cost-free source of financing. However, if you stretch amounts owed to suppliers too far, you may hurt your credit rating. If you are offered a cash discount for early payment, take it. What is the timing relationship between collections of accounts receivable and payments of accounts payable?
- *Notes Payable*. These represent loans from third parties

...sually banks) and possibly the seller of the business. You will have to pay interest on the principal of the loans. Is your debt level excessive, creating potential problems in making loan payments?

- *Accrued Expenses.* Accrued expenses represent amounts owed for expenses (e.g., utilities, interest, salaries, taxes). These are obligations of the business at the end of the accounting period. Do you have sufficient funds to pay these expenses when due?

In managing working capital, you have to consider the tradeoff between return and risk. Holding more current assets than fixed assets means less liquidity risk. It also means greater flexibility, since current assets may be modified easily as sales volume changes. However, fixed assets typically earn a greater return than current assets. Long-term financing has less liquidity risk associated with it than short-term debt, but it also carries a higher cost.

11

CASH MANAGEMENT

Cash refers to currency and demand deposits. *Cash management* involves having the optimum amount of cash on hand at the right time. Proper cash management requires that you know how much cash the business needs, as well as how much the business has, and where that cash is at all times. If you do not keep track of the money, your business may fail.

The objective of cash management is to invest excess cash for a return, while retaining sufficient liquidity to satisfy future needs. You must plan when to have excess funds available for investment and when to borrow money.

The amount of cash to be held depends upon current liquidity position, liquidity risk preferences, schedule of debt maturity, ability to borrow, forecasted cash flow, and the probabilities of different cash flows under varying circumstances. Your business should not have an excessive cash balance since no return is earned on those funds.

Cash management also requires knowing the amount of funds available for investments and the length of time for which they can be invested. When cash receipts and disbursements are highly synchronized and predictable, your business may keep a small cash balance. You must accurately forecast the amount of cash needed, its source, and its destination. Forecasting assists you in properly timing financing, debt repayment, and the amount to be transferred between accounts.

Less cash needs to be on hand when you can borrow quickly from a bank, perhaps under a *line of credit agreement,* which permits you to borrow instantly up to a specified maximum amount. A business may also find ne cash unnecessarily tied up in other accounts, such as advances to employees. Excess cash should be invested in marketable securities for a return. However, cash in some bank accounts may not be available for investment. For instance, when a bank lends money to a business, the bank often requires the firm to keep funds on hand as collateral. This deposit is called a *compensating balance,* which in effect represents *restricted* cash for the business. Further, interest is not earned on this compensating balance.

Holding marketable securities serves as protection against cash shortages. Businesses with seasonal operations may buy marketable securities when they have excess funds and then sell the securities when cash deficits occur.

The thrust of cash management is to accelerate cash receipts and delay cash payments.

Acceleration of Cash Inflow. To accelerate cash inflow, you must (1) know the bank's policy regarding fund availability, (2) know the source and location of company receipts, and (3) devise procedures for quick deposit of checks.

Cash inflow may be accelerated by having the collection center located near the customer. Local banks should be selected to speed the receipt of funds for subsequent transfer to the central account. As an alternative, strategic post office lockboxes may be used for customer remissions. The local bank collects from these boxes periodically during the day and deposits the funds in the corporate account.

Delay of Cash Outflow. There are various ways to delay cash payment, including:
- Failing to sign the check.
- Postdating the check.
- Using drafts to pay bills, since drafts are not due on demand. When a bank receives a draft, it must return the draft to you for acceptance before payment. When you accept the draft, you then deposit the funds with the bank; hence, you can maintain a smaller average checking balance.

30

- Mailing checks from locations where the mail must go through several handling points, lengthening the payment period.
- Drawing checks on remote banks so that the payment period is lengthened.
- Using credit cards and charge accounts in order to lengthen the time between the acquisition of goods and the date of payment for those goods.

Payments to vendors should be delayed to the maximum as long as there is no associated finance charge or impairment of the company's credit rating. Of course, bills should not be paid before their due dates because of the time value of money.

A business can minimize its cash balances by using probabilities related to the expected time that checks will clear. Deposits, for example, may be made to a payroll checking account based on the expected time needed for the checks to clear.

12

INVENTORY MANAGEMENT AND CONTROL

In managing inventory, you should:
- Appraise the adequacy of the inventory level, which depends on several factors, including expected sales and seasonal considerations.
- Forecast future movement in inventory prices; if prices are expected to increase, additional inventory should be purchased at the lower price.
- Discard slow-moving products to reduce inventory carrying costs and improve cash flow.
- Guard against inventory buildup, since it is associated with substantial carrying and opportunity costs.
- Minimize inventory levels when liquidity and/or inventory financing problems exist.
- Plan for a stock inventory balance that will guard against and cushion the possible loss of business from an inventory shortage.
- Examine the quality of merchandise received. In this connection, the ratio of purchase returns to purchases should be examined. A sharp increase in the ratio indicates that a new supplier may be needed.
- Keep a careful record of backorders. A high backorder level indicates that lower inventory balances are required.
- Appraise the acquisition and inventory control functions. Any problems must be identified and rectified. In areas where control is weak, inventory balances should be restricted.
- Closely supervise warehouse and handling staff to guard against theft loss and to maximize efficiency.

• Minimize the lead time in the acquisition and distribution functions. The lead time in receiving goods is determined by dividing the value of outstanding orders by the average daily purchases. This ratio may indicate whether an increase in inventory stocking is required or whether the purchasing pattern should be altered.

Inventory control is an important aspect of basic recordkeeping. Inventory control can help you see such things as turnover time and seasonal fluctuations. The basic inventory records must include: the date purchased, item purchased, location, purchase price, date sold, and sale price. These records are readily computerized, especially if they are extensive, but they must be kept current. (See Key 19, Internal Controls, for a more detailed discussion.)

You have to consider the risk associated with inventory. For example, technological, perishable, fashionable, flammable, and specialized goods usually have a high realization risk. The nature of the risk associated with the particular inventory item should be taken into account in computing the desired inventory level.

Inventory management involves a trade-off between the costs associated with keeping inventory versus the benefits of holding inventory. Higher inventory levels result in increased costs from storage, insurance, spoilage, and interest on borrowed funds needed to finance inventory acquisition. However, an increase in inventory lowers the possibility of lost sales from stockouts. Further, large volume purchases will result in greater purchase discounts.

Inventory should be counted at regular, cyclic intervals; this enables you to check inventory on an ongoing basis as well as to reconcile the book and physical amounts.

Carrying and Ordering Costs. Inventory carrying costs include those for warehousing, handling, and insurance. A provisional cost for spoilage and obsolescence should also be included in the analysis of inventory. In addition, the opportunity cost of holding inventory balances must be considered. The carrying cost per unit equals:

$$\text{Carrying cost} = \frac{Q}{2} \times C$$

where Q/2 represents average quantity and C is the carrying cost per unit.

Inventory ordering costs are the costs of placing an order and receiving the merchandise. They include freight charges and the clerical costs to place an order. The ordering cost per unit equals:

$$\text{Ordering cost} = \frac{S}{Q} \times P$$

where S = total usage
Q = quantity per order
P = cost of placing an order

The total inventory cost is therefore:

$$\frac{QC}{2} + \frac{SP}{C}$$

A trade-off exists between ordering and carrying costs. A greater order quantity will increase carrying costs but lower ordering costs.

Economic Order Quantity (EOQ). The economic order quantity (EOQ) is the optimal amount of goods to order each time an order is placed so that total inventory costs are minimized.

$$\text{EOQ} = \sqrt{\frac{2SP}{C}}$$

The number of orders to be made for a period is the usage (S) divided by the EOQ.

EXAMPLE:

A business needs to know how frequently to place its orders. The following information is provided:

S = 500 units per month

P = $40 per order
C = $4 per unit

$$EOQ = \sqrt{\frac{2SP}{C}} = \sqrt{\frac{2(500)(40)}{4}} = \sqrt{10,000} = 100 \text{ units}$$

The number of orders required each month is:

$$\frac{S}{EOQ} = \frac{500}{100} = 5$$

Therefore, an order should be placed about every six days (31/5).

Stockouts. Stockout of inventory can result in customer dissatisfaction. In order to avoid a stockout situation, a safety stock level should be maintained. Safety stock is the minimum inventory amount needed for an item, based on anticipated usage and the expected delivery time from the supplier.

Reorder Point (ROP). The reorder point is the inventory level that signals the time to reorder merchandise at the EOQ amount.

$$ROP = \text{Lead time} \times \text{Average usage per unit of time}$$

If a safety stock is needed, then add this amount to the reorder point.

EXAMPLE:
A business needs 6,400 units evenly throughout the year. There is a lead time of one week. There are 50 working weeks in the year. The safety stock is 20 units.

$$ROP = 1 \text{ week} \times \frac{6,400 + 20}{50 \text{ weeks}} = 1 \times 128 + 20 = 148 \text{ units}$$

13

CREDIT AND COLLECTION POLICY

The major decision affecting accounts receivable is the determination of the amount and terms of credit to extend to customers. The credit terms offered have a direct bearing on the associated costs and revenue to be generated from receivables. For example, tight credit terms lead to less investment in accounts receivable and lower bad debt losses, but may also result in lower sales and reduced profits.

A firm may consider offering credit to customers with a higher-than-normal risk rating. Here, the profitability on additional sales must be compared with the increase in bad debts, higher investing and collection costs, and the opportunity cost of tying up funds in receivables for a longer period of time.

Your credit policy should be flexible, depending upon the times. In good economic times, you may expand credit; in bad economic times, you may restrict it. As you extend credit, your cash flow should be adequate to support the accounts receivable, buy inventory, and pay operating expenses. Generally, a retailer requires a monthly cash flow of at least three times the balance of the receivables. A manufacturer needs adequate funds to operate during the time lag between billings and payment.

In evaluating a potential customer's ability to pay, consider the firm's integrity and financial soundness, the collateral to be pledged, and current economic conditions. The customer's financial position should be carefully analyzed by the credit department. Check the customer's references, including employer, bank, and vendors. Do not accept the salesperson's word on the credit standing of the customer. Salespeople often extend credit too freely because they are eager to make the sale!

Some sources of credit information on companies and individuals are:

- *Credit Bureaus.* There are private agencies providing credit information on business firms and individuals. Examples are TRW (800-262-7432) and the International Consumer Credit Association. Most local credit bureaus are affiliated with the Associated Credit Bureaus of America. Computerized credit reports may be obtained.
- *Mercantile Credit Agencies.* These are private agencies that gather and appraise credit information on business firms. An example is Dun and Bradstreet (516-293-1190).
- *Suppliers.* Your suppliers may furnish information on your potential customers.

You should prepare a credit application form that each customer must fill out before you give credit. Information required on the form should include length of employment, position, income, bank accounts, net worth, and other pertinent data.

The credit policy of your business may be based on the type and size of customer, product or services offered, pricing strategy, cost of the product relative to selling price, overall business strategy, liquidity position, competition, and distribution channels. In establishing a credit policy, consider the following:

- Credit limits should be revised as customer financial health changes.
- Marketing factors are critical, since an excessively restricted credit policy will lead to lost sales.
- If seasonal datings are used, the firm may offer more liberal payments than usual during slow periods in order to stimulate business by selling to customers who are unable to pay until later in the season. This policy is financially appropriate when the return on the additional sales plus the lowering in inventory costs is

greater than the incremental cost associated with the additional investment in accounts receivable.

As per the federal Truth in Lending Law, the information to be contained in credit agreements must include cash price for merchandise or services, down payment, amount being financed, method of determining the balance subject to the finance charge, annual percentage finance rate, finance charges, total payments, principal and interest portion of payments, number and amount of periodic payments, due dates of payments, penalty charges, and description of collateral.

Periodic statements showing the balances owed should be mailed to customers. The statement must include the beginning balance, purchases, customer payments, the finance charge, annual percentage rate, unpaid balance, and the closing date of the billing cycle. In many states, the minimum time before you can charge interest on a purchase is 30 days after the purchase.

In a credit card transaction, you will receive payment for the merchandise or services before the customer pays the credit card issuer. By accepting credit cards, you protect yourself against uncollectibility, because the credit card company is taking the risk, and you gain more customers because many people are credit card holders. You are assessed a fee based on the amount of each purchase charged to a credit card. Because of the recordkeeping involved, you should set minimum amounts for such purchases. On the plus side, credit card purchasers tend to spend more and are less concerned about the price of the merchandise. However, you must be careful of credit card theft and counterfeiting. Note also that the customer may stop payment on a disputed item and that there is a greater tendency to return merchandise purchased on credit cards.

You may sell seasonal merchandise by accepting installment payments over several months. Installment payment plans are useful for more expensive items, usually durable goods (e.g., furniture) that have high value and long life. If the customer fails to make payments, you may repossess the item. Because a larger down payment makes the buyer feel more like the owner, a suggested down payment is 25 percent. Also, a larger down payment and higher monthly payments protect against a decline in the value of the item if repossession is necessary. The unpaid balance should be below the market value of the item.

It pays for a firm to give a discount for early payment by customers when the return on the funds received early is greater than the cost of the discount. A term of sale may be 2/10, net/30 which means if the customer pays in 10 days he or she receives a 2 percent discount but must pay the balance in 30 days.

Your collection policy should consider the following:
- Customer statements should be mailed the day after the close of the billing period.
- Large sales should be billed immediately.
- Customers should be invoiced for goods when the order is processed rather than when it is shipped.
- Billing for services should be done on an interim basis or immediately prior to the actual services. The billing process will be more uniform if cycle billing is employed.
- Accelerated collection should be employed for customers experiencing financial problems.

You may turn a delinquent account over to a collection agency four to six months after the purchase date. Of course, a significant fee will be charged by the collection agency upon collection. You may also take a delinquent customer to court for nonpayment. If a small amount of money is involved, you may go to small claims court where a laywer is not needed and the chance of collection is high.

14

DECIDING UPON A LEGAL STRUCTURE FOR THE BUSINESS

Your business may be organized as a sole proprietorship, a partnership, or a corporation.

Sole Proprietorship. In a sole proprietorship, the easiest legal structure to establish, the business is owned and operated by one individual. You have to obtain the appropriate licenses from local governmental authorities. The advantages of a sole proprietorship compared to the other legal forms are that it has greater freedom from governmental regulation; you retain all the profit; it is less expensive to establish and easier to terminate; and you keep full control over the business. The disadvantages of a sole proprietorship are that you may have more difficulty obtaining capital; you have access to limited skills and capabilities; and you have unlimited personal liability for the firm's debts.

Partnership. In a partnership, two or more persons co-own the business. An attorney will assist in preparing the written articles of partnership specifying the terms and conditions. In a partnership, at least one partner has unlimited liability; the agreement has limited life since it ceases upon the death of one partner. Partners share in profits, and each partner is legally responsible for the acts of the other partner or partners. A partner may be active or inactive in running the affairs of the partnership. A limited partner can lose only his or her investment in the partnership, while a general partner is personally liable for all partnership debts. However, the general partner manages and controls the business.

The advantages of a partnership are that it offers flexibility in meeting changing business conditions; each partner's share of the income of the partnership is reported only on his or her personal income tax return (although the partnership has to prepare IRS Form 1065, U.S. Partnership Return of Income); each partner shares in partnership profits; there is less governmental control than for a corporation; there is additional capital available compared to a sole proprietorship; there is access to greater capabilities because more people are involved; partnerships are easier to form than corporations and provide greater stability (for instance if one partner gets sick, others are there to take his or her place) than a sole proprietorship.

The disadvantages of a partnership are that one partner is legally responsible for the actions of another partner; there may be personal power conflicts; at least one partner has unlimited liability for partnership debts; it may be difficult to buy out a problem partner; and it may be more difficult to obtain financing compared to a corporation.

Corporation. Since a corporation is the most complex structure, you should retain an attorney for the incorporation process. If the company is to do business in more than one state, federal laws must be followed with regard to interstate commerce, as must the laws of the respective states. You should be familiar with the general procedures of incorporation.

Most states have a standard certificate-of-incorporation form. The information to be filled in typically includes the name of the company, corporate objectives, name and addresses of incorporators and board of directors, location of the main office, the names of the stockholders and the type of shares each will receive, period of time for which the company is being formed (in most cases perpetual), and capital requirements.

Assuming the information contained in the certificate of incorporation is approved, a charter will be issued by the state. Most small corporations obtain their charter from the state in which the greater part of their business is conducted. However, it may be advantageous to incorporate in another state. In the state in which you are located, this would be known as a "foreign corporation." Advantages of incorporating in another state may include lower taxes, lower capital requirements, and fewer corporate restrictions. But there are drawbacks to being a foreign corporation. These include being subject to double taxation (in the state in which you reside and the state in which you are incorporated) and possibly receiving less favorable treatment of property. In addition, without certification to do business within the home state, the company may lose its right to sue in that state.

The advantages of incorporation are that it offers limited liability (the officer is not personally liable for corporate debts); it has unlimited life (the company does not cease when a principal officer retires), it provides greater ability to obtain additional financing, as well as the ability to obtain attractive fringe benefits (company cars, pension plan, insurance plan) and the use of many skills and talents among its officers. The disadvantages of incorporation are that the company is subject to double taxation (it is taxed on corporate profit and the stockholder is then again taxed on dividends received); stockholders are unable to deduct net losses of the company on their personal tax returns; the company faces increased government regulation; and there is significant recordkeeping.

State taxes and organizational fees vary among states and should be considered.

15

WHAT TO KNOW ABOUT THE LEGAL CONTRACT

You will need an attorney to represent you when negotiating and completing the purchase contract. The written legal agreement should contain the following items:
- The purchase price and the method of payment. For example, can you borrow money from the seller at a lower interest rate than the bank offers?
- The date the buyer effectively owns the business.
- A detailed description of what is being sold, including all of the assets, particularly inventory.
- The liabilities you will or will not assume.
- Seller warranties.
- Who is responsible for what expenses (e.g., bills, legal and accounting fees, payroll taxes).
- Noncompetition clause by the seller, specifying duration and geographic area.

It is best to close as soon as possible after the contract date to minimize the transitional problems and to keep the condition of the business in good working order. For example, the seller is not likely to make needed repairs between contract and closing. The seller should set up an escrow account for unexpected repairs. A quick closing also reduces the chance of inventory problems.

You may ask for a "buy-back" contract in which the seller agrees to buy back the business if you do not do well, perhaps failing to meet a specified sales or earnings objective. It is usually best to pay out the purchase price over an extended time period to assure the continued cooperation of the seller.

16

BUSINESS LICENSES

You may have to obtain various business licenses in order to operate.

You may need a license to practice a particular occupation, such as medicine or law. Contact the Department of Commerce of your state to see if you fall under this requirement.

Typically, you obtain a local business license from the municipality by contacting the city or county hall. Before such a license is issued, you may have to conform to specific zoning laws, building codes, fire protection specifications, and health regulations. When you obtain your business license, you will be notified if special permits are required.

Since the federal government regulates interstate commerce, you will need a federal license if you will sell your product in several states. Further, federal licenses and permits are required for businesses engaged in certain activities, such as common carriers and radio stations.

17

OBTAINING A PATENT, TRADEMARK, OR COPYRIGHT

You may want to patent a product, register a trademark, or obtain a copyright in order to protect what you have from competitive infringement.

Patent. Generally, only the inventor may apply for a patent from the U.S. Patent and Trademark Office. You may obtain a patent granting exclusive rights for 17 years, at a significant cost. By the time you are through with all the fees involved, it will cost you several thousand dollars.

A patent covers the invention or discovery of a *new* and *useful* process, manufacture, or composition of matter. The invention must be significantly different from any similar invention that has already been made.

It is best to retain a patent attorney or patent agent when applying for a patent because he or she is knowledgeable about the application procedures and your rights. Contact the patent office mentioned earlier in this section for a listing of registered lawyers and agents. The patent application includes a specification and description of the invention, any claims you are making about it, a drawing (where possible), and the filing fee. The specification includes the manner and process of producing and using the item.

When you produce or sell patented products, you must mark the items "patented" along with the patent number. You may sue any other business that infringes upon your patented product.

Copyright. A copyright, which runs for the holder's life plus 50 years after his or her death, is protection given an author or artist for an original work in the form of exclusive rights to the creation. Examples of items that may be copyrighted are literary works, pictorial works, motion pictures, musical works, and sound recordings.

While your copyright is valid automatically, it is recommended that you register it so there will be a public record. Registration is a prerequisite in bringing a copyright infringement case.

An author or someone deriving his or her rights may apply for copyright permission. You can do the copyright registration yourself by filling out an application, paying a small application fee, and providing a copy of the work. An application may be obtained from the Register of Copyrights, Library of Congress, Washington, D.C. 20559.

Trademark. A trademark applies to any word, symbol, name, or device used by a manufacturer to identify his or her *distinguishable* product. Registration is made with the Commissioner of Patents and Trademarks, Washington, D.C. 20231. The application includes a drawing of the mark, five specimens or facsimiles, and the application fee. Even though registration is not required for a trademark to be protected, registration is recommended so you may sue for any infringement. You are giving constructive notice of ownership. Criminal penalties are assessed to those who counterfeit a registered trademark.

A serial number will be assigned for the trademark. The notice of trademark is stated as "Registered in U.S. Patent and Trademark Office."

A trademark is good for 20 years and may be renewed for periods of 20 years from the expiration date. Between the fifth and sixth year subsequent to registration, the registrant must file an affidavit stating that the mark is currently being used in business.

18

PROTECTING AGAINST CRIMINAL ACTS

Crime is a serious problem for small businesses and may lead not only to significant financial loss but also to business failure. Crimes, including burglary, robbery, shoplifting, internal theft, and passing uncollectable checks can send your insurance rates up, or make it impossible for you to get insurance.

Shoplifting. Shoplifting is the most common crime perpetrated on small businesses. You have to try to learn how to identify a shoplifter. Shoplifters may appear clumsy or erratic in their behavior. Most shoplifters are juveniles.

Be on guard against these common shoplifting tactics:
- Putting on clothes and walking out with them.
- Switching price tags.
- Putting the item to be stolen in the shoplifter's pocket.
- Using one shoplifter as a decoy to cause a distraction while another steals.

Returned merchandise should come in a bag with the receipt. Make sure the customer has not been walking around the store before coming to the checkout counter.

Ways of deterring shoplifting are:
- Locking display cabinets containing expensive merchandise.
- Using protective equipment such as two-way mirrors, one-way viewing mirrors, peepholes, and convex wall mirrors.
- Using closed-circuit television in the cashier area and aisles.

- Stapling receipts to the outside of packages.
- Using hard-to-break plastic string.
- Having employees patrol the aisles when the store is busy.
- Posting signs warning about the penalties of shoplifting.
- Having a security guard.
- Locking doors not in use unless that would be a violation of the fire code.
- Designing the store's layout and structure to deter shoplifting by having adequate lighting, positioning the cash register where the cashier can see the aisles clearly, and having only one entrance in front of the store.
- Instructing employees on shoplifting tactics, likely shoplifters, and how to identify suspicious shoppers.
- Having an employee stationed at the dressing room. The employee may give the customer a tag showing how many garments he or she is bringing in.
- Allowing only two articles at a time into a fitting room.
- Watching for shoppers who are in the store for long time periods, those shopping during lunch, and those handling a lot of merchandise.
- Guarding against switched price labels.
- Marking merchandise with sensitized tags which cannot be removed without damaging the merchandise. If the item is taken out of the store before the tag is removed by a clerk, an alarm will sound.

Employees who spot a shoplifter should be able to alert one another by a prearranged signal or code. You have to be careful when apprehending a shoplifter, because you do not want to disturb your regular customers and you do not want to arrest an innocent party who can then sue for false arrest. (You should carry insurance for this eventuality.) In order for a shoplifting charge to succeed, you must be able to do the following:

- Positively identify the merchandise as yours.
- Testify that the person intended to steal the item.
- Prove the person did not pay for the merchandise.
- See the shoplifter take or conceal the merchandise.

If you cannot support each of the above, you will probably lose the case.

Burglary. Burglary is an unlawful entry in order to commit a theft. Ways to prevent burglary include:

- *Alarm.* A silent central station alarm is typically better than a local one with a siren. But if you want to frighten the burglar before entrance, an audio alarm is better. You can also have sensory devices such as ultrasonic, radar motion, or vibration detectors.
- *Lighting.* Lighting your premises at night will discourage burglars, who prefer darkness.
- *Key control.* Stamp the door key "Do Not Duplicate." Control over keys is necessary; give the key only to authorized users. If an employee is terminated or a key is lost, change the lock. Avoid a master key because it detracts from the overall security system. Use a code number on the key rather than a tag saying what lock it opens. Change locks periodically to prevent use of old keys by former employees.
- *Burglar-resistent windows.* The use of impact-resistant plastic windows or laminated glass will deter burglaries.
- *Burglar-resistent safes.* The "E" safe may be used. Preferably, the safe should be bolted to the building structure, be visible from the street (if possible), and be well-lit at night. You should not have the combination at the store, and when an employee leaves, the combination should be changed.
- *Locks.* The best security is the pin-tumbler cylinder lock or a double cylinder dead-bolt lock.
- *Watch dogs.*
- *Daily cash deposits.*

Robbery. Robbery is the act of taking a valuable item by using force, violence, or intimidation. This is a serious problem for retail stores. Typically, a weapon is used in a robbery.

To help prevent robberies:

- Use an armored service, where warranted.
- Do not carry money where it can obviously be seen.
- Have silent alarms, such as holdup buttons, installed.
- Carry a handgun.
- Vary your routes and hours for going to the bank so there is no consistent pattern.

- Use a surveillance camera.
- Use a dual-control safe that can be opened only by you and the armored guard.

If you receive a night call at home that something is wrong at the store, make sure you are accompanied by the police since the robber may be waiting for you.

Uncollectable Checks. Before accepting a customer's check, you should:

- Preferably know the check passer.
- Make sure the check has not been altered in any way.
- Check the amount—bad checks are statistically most common in the amounts of $25 to $35.
- Set a maximum limit for a check that you will accept.
- Compare signatures on the check and on the identification.
- Be more cautious about low serial number checks.
- See if the customer shows a lack of concern for the price of the goods.
- Refuse to accept checks dated 30 days before the purchase date.
- Require two pieces of identification. Put the serial number from the driver's license on the check. The best forms of identification are driver's license, credit cards, and automobile registration.
- Refuse to accept a personal check for more than the purchase price, cashing the difference.
  Do not accept a check if:
- The customer is acting strangely.
- The check is predated by the customer in the store.
- The check has an old date.
- The individual appears to be under the influence of alcohol or drugs.

Make sure to verify all credit cards. They may be stolen or the holder may have exceeded the maximum limit.

19

INTERNAL CONTROLS

Since employee theft is common, you should carefully screen all job applicants. Try to eliminate or minimize bad feelings about the company among employees by offering promotion, job enrichment, increasing job responsibility, and fair salaries. In addition, look to the employer's behavior as a role model; if the employer takes company-owned items for personal use, employees may emulate such behavior.

Types of employee theft include stealing company merchandise or supplies, stealing petty cash and making out false vouchers, taking kickbacks, forging a company check to one's own order and destroying the check when it is returned from the bank, stealing cash payments received by mail, and cashing company checks made out for fictitious bills to nonexistent vendors.

Having one individual in charge of a transaction from beginning to end opens up the possibility of manipulation. To reduce the incidence of employee theft:
- Watch for employees who bypass items when ringing up sales.
- Do unannounced price checks to see that pricing is correct.
- Allow only authorized employees to set prices and mark merchandise.
- Watch for a salesperson or waiter or waitress who is very popular. Is it because he or she is giving away something for free? Why do customers like the person so much? Perhaps the employee is undercharging for a better tip? Perhaps a salesperson is getting a kick-

back? Are many customers relatives or friends of the employee?

- Make sure that incoming shipments are being recorded.
- Match return vouchers to the items on the stock.
- Do not allow employees to park near the door making it easier for them to steal merchandise.
- Telephone customers with return vouchers to make sure they received the refund.

Some internal controls include:

- Retaining a CPA to audit the company's books and records.
- Separating the physical handling of an asset and the recordkeeping for it. For example, the person keeping the cash or inventory records should not have physical possession of the asset.
- Having one employee record a sale and another one charge the customer's account.
- Having one employee receive a collection and another one credit the customer's account.
- Having one employee approve invoices for payment and another one issue the checks.
- Having one employee prepare the payroll and another one issue the checks.
- Clearly stamping invoices paid.
- Having spot checks on the employees' actions.
- Having employee responsible for keeping records take periodic vacations so his or her temporary replacement can uncover any irregularities.
- Requiring multiple signatures on large dollar amount checks.
- Serially numbering checks, purchase invoices, and sales invoices.
- Matching the payee to the list of approved vendors.
- Endorsing checks "Deposit Only."
- Never making out a check to "cash" or "bearer."
- Never presigning a blank check.
- Using a modern cash register.
- Preparing bank reconciliations each month.

- Checking documentation or bills before making out checks.
- Prenumbering cash receipt documents.
- Restrictively endorsing checks received.
- Returning bank statements and deposit slips to an employee other than the one who made the deposit.
- Immediately investigating customer complaints of unfilled orders when payment was made.
- Having a periodic physical count of inventory.
- Having employees sign for stockroom items.
- Having cameras in the storage area to guard against employee theft.
- Using a card entry system in top security areas.
- Comparing purchase orders with vendor catalogues.
- Determining the accuracy of pay rates and any changes therein as well as approvals for overtime.
- Determining the proper recording of employee hours, perhaps by examining time cards.
- Determining the improper changing of an amount.
- Personally approving unusual discounts or bad debt writeoffs.

A common form of employee theft is embezzlement, in which cash received is pocketed by the employee without recording the sale. The following occurrences may indicate that embezzlement has taken place:

- Inventory shortages.
- Slow collection.
- Delays in depositing cash.
- Frequent cash shortages among employees.
- A drop or an unusually small increase in cash or credit sales. Perhaps sales are not being recorded.
- A drop in profit, indicating that cash may be taken and/or accounts manipulated.
- Unusual activity in an inactive account.
- Unusual bad debt writeoffs. Perhaps the money was collected but the account was written off anyway.
- Increase in sales returns, indicating that accounts receivable payments are being concealed.

Encourage employees to tell you about their personal

ıd financial problems. Then you will know who might experiencing some difficulty and who might therefore be vulnerable to temptation.

You can also hire "shopper detectives" who pose as customers to see if employees act honestly and professionally. For example, does the waiter undercharge in hopes of a better tip?

20

ACCOUNTING
RECORDS

You should not mix up your personal and business records; you need a separate bank account for your business. Remember, you can take off only business-related items for tax purposes.

Do not wait until you are licensed or open for business to keep records; begin as soon as you start to refine your ideas. There are many people who have wonderful ideas for products or services who do not want to be bothered with the boring details of recordkeeping—their businesses are doomed to failure. A competent bookkeeper should be hired, and a CPA should be retained to audit your records periodically and to prepare the necessary financial reports and tax returns.

The records you keep serve two functions. The first is documenting activity for tax purposes, and the second is enabling you to see the trends in your business and take appropriate action where necessary to improve (or save) it. The accounting records enable you to monitor financial condition and operating performance. They tell how you are doing financially.

Without accurate, current information, you cannot make well-reasoned business decisions. As your company grows, you must stop depending on your memory and the notes you jot down and instead set up a system for compiling, recording, and analyzing business data. The accounting information needed by a company will vary with its size and amount of trade and the ability of the owner to use such information. Without adequate and carefully prepared records, it is impossible for a modern small business to handle buying and selling, inventory control, credit and collection, expense control, personnel, production control, and most other aspects of business management.

An adequate financial recordkeeping system will either provide the required information or assist the small firm operator in obtaining answers to such basic questions as the following:

- How does my profit this year compare to last year? How am I doing relative to my competition?
- How can I get my profit up? Are there any expenses that are too high?
- What is my net worth? What do I owe? What do I own?
- How is my cash flow?
- How much do my customers owe me? How long past due are the payments?

A small business typically has the option of being on the cash basis or accrual basis. The cash basis recognizes revenue and expenses only when the related cash is received and disbursed. Thus, recognition of transactions is tied to cash flow. However, the cash basis is an inappropriate accounting method when considerable inventory exists. Under accrual accounting, revenue is recognized when it is earned and expenses are recorded when they are incurred. Many small businesses use the cash basis because it is easier, involves less recordkeeping, and is more flexible.

Original (source) documents are the basis for recording transactions in the journals as described below. Documents include sales slips, purchase invoices, and expense bills.

If possible, disbursements should be made by check so that expenses can be documented for accounting and tax purposes. If a cash payment is necessary, a receipt for the payment, or at least an explanation of it, should be included in the records. All cancelled checks, paid bills, purchase invoices, sales slips, duplicate deposit slips, cash register tapes, and other documents that substantiate the entries in the financial records should be filed and stored in a safe place.

Business transactions are recorded in journals from information in the source documents. Journals are formal books of original entry with transactions entered daily in chronological order. Thus, the journals reflect in one place information about all financial transactions, including cash receipts, cash disbursements, sales, purchases, sales returns, purchase returns, and general activities.

The Cash Receipts Journal contains a daily listing of all incoming cash such as that from sales, collections on account, interest income, dividend income, and sales of assets. The name of the payor and reason for payment are given.

The Cash Disbursements Journal has a daily listing of all outgoing cash. This listing is in addition to, not in place of, the information in the stubs of the owner's checkbook. Cash disbursements include payments on expenses, purchases, acquisitions of assets, etc. It lists the payee, reason for payment, and check number.

The Sales Journal contains a daily listing of credit sales, including the names of the customers. Sales may be broken down by major type of marketing segment (e.g., retail sales, wholesale sales).

The Purchase Journal has a daily listing of the purchases and names of vendors.

There is also a Sales Returns and Allowances Journal and a Purchase Returns and Allowances Journal.

The General Journal provides a daily listing of all other transactions not in a separate journal. For example, you would record the uncollectibility of a customer's account in that journal.

Data are transferred from the journal to the ledger by debiting and crediting the particular accounts involved. This process is termed *posting*.

All accounts of a business are kept in the ledger, which is a separate book. The ledger, in effect, classifies and summarizes financial transactions and is the basis for the preparation of the balance sheet and income statement. It is also useful for decision making because it provides the owner with the balance in a given account at a particular time. For example, if business seems poor, the owner can determine the sales for the reporting period or the ending inventory balance. Similarly, the owner will want to know the cash balance at the end of the reporting period in order to determine whether adequate funds are on hand to meet operating requirements.

Businesses that utilize computers may store the accounts on magnetic disks rather than in a ledger binder.

In the general ledger, control accounts exist for accounts receivable and accounts payable. There are separate accounts receivable and accounts payable ledgers to show the individual customer and vendor accounts. For example, the total customer balances in the subsidiary accounts receivable ledger should equal the accounts receivable control account in the general ledger.

The accounts receivable ledger allows the owner to keep track of the money owed him or her. It should include the account name and number, invoice date and number, amount, terms of sale, amount paid, and balance. At the end of the period, statements are mailed to all open accounts.

The accounts payable ledger lists the balances owed vendors and how long they are outstanding.

Single-entry bookkeeping, although not as complete as double-entry bookkeeping, may be used effectively in the small business, especially during the early years. The single-entry system is relatively simple. The flow of income and expense is recorded through summaries of cash receipts and cash payments (as in a checkbook).

A Petty Cash Record should be kept for all noncheck purchases and payments for miscellaneous, minor amount items, such as postage, taxi fare, or minor supplies. A check is drawn to fill the petty cash fund. As cash is paid from it, a voucher is issued. At the end of the period, the Petty Cash fund is replenished.

The payroll records provide information such as employee name, social security number, address, pay rate, hours worked, overtime, gross salary, deductions, and net pay. This record provides the basis for the preparation of federal, state, and local tax returns.

21

FINANCIAL STATEMENTS

Financial statements are important because they serve as the basis on which bankers decide whether to lend you money, suppliers determine whether to give you credit, and potential investors decide whether to invest in your business. Financial statements are also very important so that you know how your business is doing financially. The two major financial statements are the income statement and balance sheet. These financial statements summarize the voluminous data contained in the detailed accounting records. Financial statements show your profit, what you own, what you owe, and how much equity you have in the business. The financial statements reveal your financial health and operating performance.

You should keep records (other than for tax purposes) so that you can see the trends in your business and make necessary changes. Businesspersons who take the time to understand and evaluate their business through financial statements will be ahead of those who concern themselves only with the products and/or services.

Income Statement. The measure of operating performance is the net income (profit) earned for the reporting period. This is shown in the *income statement,* also called profit and loss (P&L) statement.

The profit is derived by subtracting *total expenses* from *total revenue (income).* The income statement breaks down each major type of revenue and expense. This breakdown is needed, among other reasons, so that the owner can determine the trend in revenue and expense items. For example, the owner would like to know if a given expense item (e.g., telephone) is disproportionately great so that he or she can determine the reasons why and possibly control that expense item.

Revenue is the increase in capital arising from the sale of merchandise (as in a retail business) or the performance of services (as by a beautician). Earned revenue results in an increase in either Cash or Accounts Receivable.

Expenses decrease capital and result from performing those functions necessary to generate revenue. The amount of an expense is equal either to the cost of the inventory sold, the value of the services rendered (e.g., salary expense), or the expenditures necessary for conducting business operations (e.g., rent expense) during the period.

Net income is the amount by which total revenue exceeds total expenses for the reporting period. The resulting profit is added to the owner's capital. However, if total expenses are greater than total revenue, a net loss ensues and decreases the owner's capital.

It should be noted that revenue does not necessarily mean receipt of cash and expense does not automatically imply a cash payment. Net income and net cash flow (cash receipts less cash payments) are different. For example, taking out a bank loan will generate cash, but this is not revenue since merchandise has not been sold nor have services been provided. Further, capital has not been altered because of the loan.

Balance Sheet. The measure of your net worth is owner's capital (the difference between your total assets and total liabilities) at the end of the period. *Assets, liabilities* and *capital* are reported in the *balance sheet.* Each type of asset, liability, and capital account is listed so that the proprietor knows the specific items he or she owns (i.e, cash, inventory, automobile), what is owed (i.e., accounts payable, loans payable), and the amount of ending equity in the business (capital account). The equity at the end of the period consists of the capital investments made plus the profits earned less any withdrawals.

A *classified* balance sheet generally breaks down assets into four categories: current assets; long-term investments; property, plant, and equipment (fixed assets); and intangible assets.

Current assets are those assets that are expected to be converted into cash or used up within one year. Examples of current assets are cash, accounts receivable, and inventory.

Long-term investments refer to investments in other companies' stocks (common or preferred) or bonds where the *intent* is to hold them for a period greater than one year. Note that if the intent is to hold given securities for one year or less, they should be included in the current asset category and listed as short-term investments (marketable securities).

Property, plant, and equipment are assets employed in the production of goods or services and having a life greater than one year. They are tangible in nature, which means that they have physical substance (i.e., you can physically see and touch them); examples are land, buildings, machinery, and automobiles. These assets are actually being used; unlike inventory, they are not being held for sale in the normal course of business.

Intangible assets are assets with a long-term life that lack physical substance, such as goodwill, or arise from a right granted by the government, such as patents, copyrights, and trademarks, or by another company, such as franchise fees.

Liabilities may be classed as either current or noncurrent. *Current liabilities* are due within one year and will be satisfied out of current assets. Examples are accounts payable, short-term notes payable, and accrued liabilities. *Accrued liabilities* are defined as obligations from expenses incurred but not paid at the end of the reporting period. Salaries payable and telephone payable are examples. *Noncurrent liabilities* are due after a period greater than one year. Examples of long-term liabilities are a two-year note payable and a mortgage payable.

Capital equals total assets less total liabilities.

22

FINANCIAL STATEMENT ANALYSIS

Financial statement analysis is an evaluation of both a firm's past financial performance and its prospects for the future. Typically, it involves an analysis of the firm's financial statements and its flow of funds. Financial statement analysis involves the calculation of various ratios and reveals to the business owner how the business is doing, its financial health, and what areas need to be improved upon.

The owner may use ratios to make two types of comparisons:

1. *Industry comparison.* The ratios of the business are compared with those of similar businesses or with industry norms to determine how the business is faring relative to its competitors. Industry norms may be published by financial services and trade magazines.

2. *Trend analysis.* A firm's present ratio is compared with its past and expected future ratios to determine whether the company's financial condition is improving or deteriorating over time (e.g., five years).

After completing the financial statement analysis, the owner should evaluate his or her plans and prospects, any problem areas identified in the analysis, and possible solutions.

Financial ratios can be classified into four groups: liquidity ratios, activity ratios, leverage ratios, and profitability ratios.

Liquidity Ratios. Liquidity is the ability of the business to meet its maturing short-term obligations. Liquidity is essential to conducting business activity, particularly in time of adversity, such as when a business is shut down by a strike or when operating losses ensue due to a recession. If liquidity is insufficient to cushion such losses, serious financial difficulty may result.

Current Ratio. The current ratio is equal to current assets divided by current liabilities. This ratio, which is subject to seasonal fluctuations, is used to measure the ability of the business to meet its current liabilities out of current assets. A high ratio is needed when the firm has difficulty borrowing on short notice.

$$\text{Current Ratio} = \text{Current Assets/Current Liabilities}$$

Quick (Acid-Test) Ratio. The quick ratio, also known as the acid-test ratio, is a stringent test of liquidity. It is found by dividing the most liquid current assets (cash, marketable securities, and accounts receivable) by current liabilities.

$$\text{Quick Ratio} =$$
$$\text{Cash} + \text{Marketable Securities} + \text{Accounts Receivable/Current Liabilities}$$

Activity (Asset Utilization) Ratios. Activity ratios are used to determine how quickly various accounts are converted into sales or cash.

Accounts Receivable Ratios. Accounts receivable ratios consist of the accounts receivable turnover ratio and the average collection period. The *accounts receivable turnover ratio* gives the number of times accounts receivable is collected during the year. It is found by dividing net credit sales by the average accounts receivable. *Average accounts receivable* is found by adding the beginning and ending accounts receivable and dividing by 2. In general, the higher the accounts receivable turnover, the better, since the business is collecting quickly from customers and these funds can then be invested. However, an excessively high ratio may indicate that the company's credit policy is too stringent and that the business is not tapping the potential for profit through sales to customers in higher risk classes. Note that here, too, before changing its credit policy, a business has to weigh the profit potential against the risk inherent in selling to more marginal customers.

$$\text{Accounts Receivable Turnover} = \text{Net Credit Sales/Average Accounts Receivable}$$

The *collection period* (days sales in receivables) is the number of days it takes to collect on receivables.

$$\text{Average Collection Period} = 365/\text{Accounts Receivable Turnover}$$

One possible cause for the increase in the accounts receivable turnover ratio may be that the business is now selling to highly marginal customers. The owner should compare the company's credit terms with the extent to which customer balances are delinquent. An *aging schedule,* which lists the accounts receivable according to the length of time they are outstanding, is helpful for this comparison.

Inventory Ratios. If a business is holding excess inventory, funds that could be invested elsewhere for a return are tied up in inventory. In addition, there are high carrying cost for storing the goods, as well as the risk of obsolescence. On the other hand, if inventory is too low, the company may lose customers because it has run out of merchandise. Two major ratios for evaluating inventory are *inventory turnover* and *average age of inventory*.

$$\text{Inventory turnover} = \text{Cost of Goods Sold/Average Inventory}$$

$$\text{Average Age of Inventory} = 365/\text{Inventory Turnover}$$

Operating Cycle. The operating cycle is the number of days it takes to convert inventory and accounts receivable to cash. A short operating cycle is desirable.

$$\text{Operating Cycle} = \text{Average Age of Inventory} + \text{Average Collection Period}$$

Total Asset Turnover. The total asset turnover ratio is helpful in evaluating the ability of the business to use its asset base efficiently to generate revenue. A low ratio may result from many factors, and it is important to identify the underlying reasons.

Total Asset Turnover = Net Sales/Average Total Assets

Leverage (Solvency) Ratios. *Solvency* is the ability of the business to meet its long-term obligations as they become due. An analysis of solvency concentrates on the long-term financial and operating structure of the business. The degree of long-term debt in the capital structure is also considered. Further, solvency is dependent upon profitability, since in the long run a business will not be able to meet its debts unless it is profitable.

Debt Ratio. The debt ratio compares total liabilities (total debt) to total assets. It shows the percentage of total funds obtained from creditors.

Debt Ratio = Total Liabilities/Total Assets

Times Interest Earned (Interest Coverage) Ratio. The times interest earned ratio reflects the number of times before-tax earnings cover interest expense. It is a safety margin indicator in the sense that it shows how much of a decline in earnings a business can absorb.

Interest Coverage =
Earnings before Interest and Taxes/Interest Expense

Profitability Ratios. An indication of good financial health and the effectiveness with which the business is being managed is the ability of the business to earn a satisfactory profit and return on investment.

Gross Profit Margin. The gross profit margin reveals the percentage of each dollar left over after the business has paid for its goods. The higher the gross profit earned, the better. Gross profit equals net sales less cost of goods sold.

$$\text{Gross Profit Margin} = \text{Gross Profit/Net Sales}$$

Profit Margin. The ratio of net income to net sales is called the profit margin. It indicates the profitability generated from revenue and hence is an important measure of operating performance. It also provides clues to pricing and cost structure.

Return on Investment. Return on investment (ROI) is a key, but rough, measure of performance. It shows the profitability generated on assets.

$$\text{Return on Investment} = \text{Net Income/Average Total Assets}$$

Residual Income. This is a profitability measure taking into account the opportunity cost of tying up funds in the business.

$$\text{Residual Income} =$$
$$\text{Net Income} - (\text{Minimum Return} \times \text{Total Assets})$$

23

BUDGETING

A budget is a quantitative expression of a plan of action for accomplishing goals and an aid to coordination and implementation. Budgets are the vehicle for controlling your business from a financial standpoint. Statements record history while budgets make it! The budget is helpful in making two broad types of decisions: (a) operating decisions (those concerning the acquisition and utilization of resources), and (b) financial decisions (those related to obtaining funds for acquisition of resources).

A budget is a starting point for planning. You can base projections on historical patterns but must take into account any important changes in the current environment, such as new laws or increased competition. The budget may be the basis for planning sales and market share, inventory, or staff requirements. The period for a budget can be any appropriate time frame such as a year, a quarter, a month, a week, or a day.

The use of budgets forces entrepreneurs to quantify their dreams and directly face the uncertainties of their ventures. Whether the budget is properly thought out and prepared may determine the success or failure of the small business. For example, a small business with lofty hopes moved into a lush market for school equipment. However, failure to quantify the long collection period, to forecast a maximum sales potential, and to control cost from the outset resulted in disaster within a year.

In the competitive environment of small businesses, the importance of budgeting and forecasting cannot be overemphasized. They provide the opportunity to appraise the overall operation for the coming year through an evaluation of the company's strengths and weaknesses and to plan strategies.

A budget begins by forecasting sales, then production, cost of sales, and operating expenses. You should estimate the level of assets required to support the projected sales. After that, you must determine financing needs.

The master budget is classified broadly into two categories—the *operating budget* and the *financial budget*. The operating budget reflects the results of operating decisions. It provides data needed to prepare a budgeted income statement. The operating budget consists of the sales budget, purchase budget, selling and administrative expense budget, and pro forma income statement. The financial budget shows the financial decisions of the company and includes the cash budget and the pro forma balance sheet.

The sales budget is the beginning point in preparing the master budget, since estimated sales volume influences nearly all other items. The sales budget ordinarily indicates the expected sales of each product. After sales volume has been estimated, the sales budget is constructed by multiplying the expected unit sales by the expected unit selling price. Based on the sales budget, you can plan your needs. Further, sales forecast figures determine staffing requirements for reaching targeted goals.

After the sales budget comes the purchase budget, in which you determine how much you have to buy and what you want in inventory. The purchases depend on the quantity needed to support the sales base and the unit purchase price.

The selling and administrative expense budget lists the operating expenses incurred in selling the products and in managing the business.

The budgeted income statement summarizes the various component projections of revenue and expenses for the budgeting period.

In preparing a cash budget, you add to the beginning cash balance the expected cash receipts to obtain the total amount available to spend. You then subtract cash payments, leaving the ending cash balance.

The cash budget usually comprises the following four major sections:

1. The receipts section, which gives the beginning cash balance, cash collections from customers, and other receipts (e.g., from borrowing money or selling assets). Note that cash receipts are not necessarily the same as revenue (e.g., credit sales).

2. The disbursements section, which shows all cash payments, listed by purpose. Examples are cash expenses, purchase of assets, and payment of debt. Note that not all expenses are cash payments (e.g., depreciation).

3. The cash surplus or deficit section, which simply shows the difference between the cash receipts section and the cash disbursements section and tells you how much of a cash surplus or deficit you have.

4. The financing section, which provides a detailed account of the borrowings and repayments expected during the budget period.

A cash budget reveals whether cash on hand will be sufficient to meet your needs. Because the cash budget details the expected cash receipts and disbursements for a designated time period, it helps avoid the problem of either having idle cash on hand or suffering a cash shortage. If a cash shortage is experienced, the cash budget indicates whether the shortage is temporary or permanent, i.e., whether short-term or long-term borrowing is needed. When will there be peak cash needs? Is a line of credit necessary? Should capital expenditures and expenses be cut back? When do you have to repay debts, and will there be enough cash to do so? If the cash position is very poor, the company may even go out of business because it cannot pay its bills. If the cash position is excessive, profitable possibilities may be forgone.

The budgeted balance sheet is developed by beginning with the balance sheet for the year just ended and adjusting it, using all the activities that are expected to occur during the budgeting period. There are several reasons why the budgeted balance sheet is prepared: disclosing possible unfavorable financial conditions that you may want to avoid, helping you perform a variety of ratio calculations, and highlighting future resources and obligations.

At the end of the period, the budget is a control device to measure your performance against the plan to see how you did. You will be able to spot areas requiring correction so that future performance may be improved.

24

COSTS OF A BUSINESS

To estimate the costs of starting and operating the business, you should specify capital, startup, fixed, variable, and semivariable costs. You have to determine if you have the cash flow and resources needed to meet your costs and stay afloat. Look what happened to Donald Trump—he defaulted on his interest payments to bondholders and banks. You cannot get in over your head! Further, you have to obtain sufficient sales volume to cover ongoing expenses.

To be successful in business, you should know what it costs to produce and sell your items or render services. In this way, you can monitor and control these costs. In addition, you can formulate a reasonable selling price for your product or service. If your selling price is below cost, you will incur a loss.

You should be familiar with the types of costs and cost behavior. What are your total costs and cost per unit of product or service?

Capital outlays for your new business include property, plant and equipment, paving, landscaping, parking lots, fixtures, security systems (e.g., safe, burglar alarm), displays, and signs.

Startup costs include advertising for the opening, architect fees, real estate commission, professional fees (e.g., accountant, attorney), and building permits.

You should try to find ways to reduce your cash outflow. For example, if you can work out of your home, you avoid paying rent. Also, rather than hiring salespeople, try to use sales representatives until the commissions they earn exceed the cost of hiring and employing your own salespeople.

In general, for inexperienced businesspeople, a strict estimate of startup costs should be multiplied by a safety factor of at least two. This number should then be multiplied by a time factor reflecting the company's operating expenses for a minimum of a year. Note that these factors will vary from industry to industry. However, the guidelines will remain the same—startup costs multiplied by some safety factor and operating costs covering a certain startup time period.

If you are running a manufacturing business, you will incur manufacturing and nonmanufacturing costs. *Manufacturing costs* are those incurred in producing a product and consist of direct material, direct labor, and factory overhead. Direct material, such as cloth used to make a shirt, becomes an integral part of the finished product. Direct labor is labor involved in making the product; an example is the wages of assembly workers on an assembly line. Factory overhead includes all costs of manufacturing except direct material and direct labor; examples are depreciation, rent, taxes, insurance, and fringe benefits.

Nonmanufacturing costs (operating expenses) are expenses related to the period rather than producing the product. The two categories of operating expenses are selling and general and administrative. Selling expenses are incurred to obtain the sale (e.g., advertising, sales commission, salesperson salaries) or distributing the product to the customer (e.g., delivery charges). Selling costs may be analyzed for reasonableness by product, territory, customer class, distribution outlet, and method of sale. How good are your order-getting and order-filling activities? Marketing costs should be evaluated based on distribution methods such as direct selling to retailers and wholesalers as well as mail order sales. The second kind of nonmanufacturing costs, general and administrative expenses, are incurred in performing administrative activities and activities that affect the company as a whole. Examples are executive salaries and legal expenses.

From a planning and control standpoint, perhaps the most important way to classify costs is by how they behave in accordance with changes in volume or some measure of activity. By behavior, costs can be classified into three basic categories.

1. *Fixed Cost.* This is a total cost that remains constant regardless of activity, such as rent, property taxes, and insurance. As sales increase, fixed costs do not increase. In consequence, profits can increase rapidly during good times. But during bad times fixed costs do not decline as sales fall off, so profits fall rapidly.
2. *Variable Cost.* This refers to a total cost that varies directly with changes in activity (e.g., direct material, direct labor, sales commissions, warranties, repairs, office supplies). Thus, a 20 percent increase in variable cost accompanies a 20 percent increase in sales.
3. *Semivariable (Mixed) Cost.* This is a cost that is part fixed and part variable. Examples are telephone and electricity bills and rental of a car or truck with a fixed rental fee plus a variable charge based on mileage.

Assuming your company has idle capacity (is not using all its capacity), the cost behavior relationships of fixed cost, variable cost, and semivariable cost are shown in Exhibit 1.

EXHIBIT 1
COST BEHAVIOR

	Unit Cost	Total Cost
Fixed	Up/Down to Volume	Constant
Variable	Constant	Up/Down to Volume
Semivariable	Up/Down to Volume	Up/Down to Volume

EXAMPLE:
Your company is operating at idle capacity. Current production is 100,000 units. Total fixed cost is $100,000, and variable cost per unit is $3. If production increases to 110,000 units, the following results:

a. Total fixed cost is still $100,000.
b. Fixed cost per unit is $.91 ($100,000/110,000 units).
c. Total variable cost is $330,000.

d. Variable cost per unit is $3.

Exhibit 2 illustrates the cost behavior for a fixed cost, such as rent.

EXHIBIT 2
COST BEHAVIOR FOR RENT

Volume	Rent	Unit Cost
100,000	$100,000	$1.00
150,000	100,000	.67
200,000	100,000	.50

EXHIBIT 3
COST BEHAVIOR FOR COMMISSIONS

Volume	Commissions	Unit Cost
100,000	$10,000	$.10
150,000	15,000	.10
200,000	20,000	.10

You can estimate total cost of a product or service by combining the fixed cost and variable cost.

EXAMPLE:

The estimated units for product line X is 100. The fixed cost is $600, and the variable cost is $2.25 per unit. The total cost is:

Fixed cost	$600	
Variable cost	225	(100 × $2.25)
Total cost	$825	

You may determine average cost per unit (or service) by dividing total cost by total units (or service hours). For example, if total cost is $10,000 for the production of 1,000 units, the average cost is $10 per unit.

There is other cost terminology you should be familiar with in operating a small business:

• *Incremental cost* is the difference in costs between two or more alternatives. For example, if the direct labor costs to produce products A and B are $10,000 and $15,000, respectively, the incremental cost is $5,000.

• *Sunk cost* is a cost that has already been incurred and will therefore not change regardless of which alternative is chosen. It represents past costs. An example is the $50,000 cost of a machine paid for three years ago which now has a book value of $20,000. The $20,000 book value is a sunk cost which does not affect a future decision.

- *Relevant cost* is the expected cost difference between alternatives. The incremental cost is relevant to a decision but the sunk cost is not.
- *Opportunity cost* is the net revenue forgone by rejecting an alternative. For example, if you have the choice of using your department's capacity to produce an extra 10,000 units or renting it out for $20,000, the opportunity cost of using the capacity is $20,000.
- *Discretionary cost* is a cost that can be discontinued without affecting the accomplishment of essential business objectives in the short-run (e.g., bonuses).

25

COST ANALYSIS

Cost is basically an expenditure incurred to obtain revenue. Cost information is useful in planning and budgetary decisions as well as in gauging performance. Are your budgeted costs sufficient to meet your needs? How do your expected costs compare to your actual costs? What are the reasons for any deviation?

Cost information should be provided to the extent it provides a benefit in the decision-making process. It is important to know the costs associated with a product, service, or activity for operational and control purposes.

Cost analysis provides many benefits including determining profitability and aiding in cost control. Further, you should compare actual costs with budgeted costs for efficiency evaluation. You should determine the costs by product, territory, and salesperson to monitor performance. Cost estimates may be made for alternative methods of selling products. For example, to find the best approach you might compare the effect of distributing samples with the effect of media advertising.

Cost information serves many purposes. It can assist in determining the minimum order you should accept; your profit by product, territory, and customer; and the desirability of servicing particular types of accounts through jobbers or telephone and mail order. In addition, it can help you decide which supplier to deal with based on the total cost of buying the merchandise, including any transportation charges.

Cost information for advertising programs aids in making decisions for future media communications. Special cost structures may be formulated for market test cases to examine cost effectiveness. The optimal method is the one providing the sales volume with the best return on investment.

You should analyze entertainment expense by customer, salesperson, or territory. Are expenses in line with the revenue obtained? In appraising entertainment expense, consider the cost per dollar of net sales and the cost per customer. Are these costs reasonable?

It is useful to know for control purposes the following costs so proper action may be taken: cost per order received, cost per order filled, cost per customer account, and cost per item handled.

In evaluating the auto expense associated with salespeople, you should consider for reasonableness both cost per month and cost per mile.

Material costs per unit may drop as a result of quantity discounts and changes in the suppliers' freight charges and terms. Material costs may also change if you substitute different materials, change suppliers, or buy different quality material. Further, direct labor costs per unit may decline because of increased worker experience in performing the task. Also, new material waste will decline as increased maturity in the operation develops.

Compare marketing costs to sales by product, customer, and distribution outlet; a rising ratio may be a negative sign.

Ascertain if large percentages of customers, orders, or products generate only a small proportion of revenue. In that case, your marketing costs may be proportionately high because you have low volume business with high marketing costs. Your marketing expense often increases in proportion to the number of customers, orders, and products instead of in proportion to dollar sales. Hence, the marketing expenses may be generating only a small fraction of sales and gross profit.

If your costs, including manufacturing, selling, delivery, order processing, handling, and storage, exceed the sales generated from a particular account, you may want to cease business to that account because you are losing money. On the other hand, even if you are not making money on a product, you may decide to keep it because it opens the door for you to sell other products.

You may have to decide whether to replace an old

asset with a new one. Perhaps the old asset is costing a lot more to run then the benefit being realized from it. The factors to consider in a replacement decision include cash outlay for the new asset, net cash flow generated by the new versus old, safety and reliability of the new asset, difference in profitability and sales generated by each asset, increased efficiency and productivity for the new asset, remaining life of the old asset, tax effect, and technological advances in the new asset.

26

WHAT IS YOUR BREAK-EVEN POINT?

Before your business can realize a profit, you must first understand the concept of breaking even. To break even on your products and/or services, you must be able to calculate the sales volume needed to cover your costs and how to use this information to your advantage. You must also be familiar with how your costs react to changes in volume and how a price change affects your profits. Further, you must know what effect expense reductions will have.

Break-even is the calculation of the sales needed to cover your costs so that there is zero profit or loss. By knowing the break-even point, you know which products and/or services to emphasize and which to de-emphasize (perhaps even to drop). This knowledge allows you to improve operating results and facilitates planning because you know how much you must sell of a new item even before you introduce it.

The assumptions of break-even analysis follow:
- Selling price is constant.
- There is only one product or a constant sales mix.
- Manufacturing efficiency is constant.
- Inventories do not significantly change from period to period.
- Variable cost per unit is constant.

The guidelines for breaking even are these:
- An increase in selling price lowers break-even sales.
- An increase in variable cost increases break-even sales.
- An increase in fixed cost increases break-even sales.

Your objective, of course, is not just to break even but to earn a profit. In deciding which products to push, continue as is, or discontinue, the break-even point is not the only important factor; economic conditions, supply and demand, and the long-term impact on customer relations must also be considered. You can extend break-even analysis to concentrate on a desired profit objective.

The break-even point equals

$$S = VC + FC$$

where S = sales, VC = variable cost, and FC = fixed cost. This approach allows you to solve for break-even sales or for other unknowns as well. An example is selling price. If you want a desired before-tax profit, solve for P in the following equation:

$$S = VC + FC + P$$

EXAMPLE 1:

A product has a fixed cost of \$270,000 and a variable cost of 70 percent of sales. The break-even sales figure is

$$\begin{aligned}
S &= FC + VC \\
1S &= \$270{,}000 + .7S \\
0.3S &= \$270{,}000 \\
S &= \$900{,}000
\end{aligned}$$

If selling price per unit is \$100, break-even units are 9,000 (\$900,000/\$100). If desired profit is \$40,000, the sales needed to obtain that profit (P) are

$$\begin{aligned}
S &= FC + VC + P \\
1S &= \$270{,}000 + 0.7S + \$40{,}000 \\
0.3S &= \$310{,}000 \\
S &= \$1{,}033{,}333
\end{aligned}$$

EXAMPLE 2:

Selling price per unit \$30, variable cost per unit \$20, fixed cost \$400,000. Break-even units (u) are

$$S = FC + VC$$
$$\$30U = \$400,000 + \$20U$$
$$\$10U = \$400,000$$
$$U = 40,000$$

Break-even dollars are
40,000 units $\times$ \$30 = \$1,200,000

EXAMPLE 3:

You sell 800,000 units of an item. The variable cost is
\$2.50 per unit. Fixed cost totals \$750,000. The selling
price per unit should be \$3.44 to break even.

$$S = FC + VC$$
$$800,000\ SP = \$750,000 + \$2.50\ (800,000)$$
$$800,000\ SP = \$2,750,000$$
$$SP = \$3.44$$

EXAMPLE 4:

The following information is given regarding a product: selling price \$40, variable cost \$24, fixed cost
\$150,000, after-tax profit \$240,000, and tax rate 40 percent.

You wish to know how many units to sell to earn the
after-tax profit.

$$S = FC + VC + P$$
$$\$40U = \$150,000 + \$24\ U + \$400,000^{(a)}$$
$$\$16U = \$550,000$$
$$U = 34,375\ units$$

$^{(a)}$0.6 $\times$ before-tax profit = after-tax profit
0.6 before-tax profit = \$240,000
Before-tax profit = $\dfrac{\$240,000}{0.6}$ = \$400,000

EXAMPLE 5:

The following data are given about a product: selling

81

price $50, variable cost $30, sales volume 60,000 units, fixed cost $150,000, and tax rate 30 percent.

You wish to determine the after-tax profit.

$$S = FC + VC + P$$
$$(\$50 \times 60{,}000) = \$150{,}000 + (\$30 \times 60{,}000) + P$$
$$\$1{,}050{,}000 = P$$
$$\text{After-tax profit} = \$1{,}050{,}000 \times 0.70 = \$735{,}000$$

27

CHOOSING THE FISCAL YEAR

As a new business owner, you will have to select a fiscal year. Most sole proprietorships and partnerships report on a January-to-December year because each individual also reports and pays taxes on that basis. A newly-formed corporation makes the initial election simply by closing its first year at the end of any month it selects. An existing company may change its reporting year by seeking approval from the Internal Revenue Service.

A corporation may elect to report on a noncalendar fiscal year for a number of reasons. First, such a basis may conform to the natural business cycle. Many retail businesses experience the majority of their sales from August to September or from November to December. Contractors are typically more active in the spring and summer. Many service organizations are subject to their own seasonal swings. Accountants may encourage their clients to select a noncalendar reporting year for their convenience; accountants are busiest in the first calendar quarter, when most closings and tax reporting occur, and would prefer to have some clients end their years in less hectic periods.

While your accountant's preferences is not an acceptable reason to request a change in fiscal year, it may still be logical to do so. There may be a benefit for closing the accounting period based on the seasonal nature of the business; your accountant may also have more time to serve your needs in a period other than when taxes and audits make demands on his or her time.

28

INDIVIDUAL AND PARTNERSHIP TAXES

You have to pay income taxes on the profit from your business. If you are a sole proprietor, your profit or loss is reported on Schedule C (Profit or Loss from Business or Profession) on your personal income tax return, IRS Form 1040. Schedule C contains a space for your social security number, employer identification number, your principal business or profession, gross income, expenses, and net profit (loss). Since you can deduct the losses from your business on the tax return, you are able to reduce your other personal income.

There are "start-up" tax breaks to acquiring or starting your own business. Although the initial expenses in connection with a *preliminary* investigation of a business (e.g., accounting and legal advice, travel) are typically not deductible, once you *concentrate* on a particular business, you may deduct the startup costs. Such costs are amortized (prorated) equally over at least five years. The deduction is claimed on Form 4562. You have to attach a statement describing the expenses incurred including when incurred, the date the business started, and the amortization period.

The expenses that may be amortized include professional services, advertising, training, consulting, evaluating potential markets and products, surveying the labor supply, examining transportation facilities, and travel costs to visit potential suppliers or customers. Even if you abandon the specific venture, you may be able to deduct a capital loss.

If the business is a partnership, you have to file a

partnership tax return (Form 1065) reflecting the revenue and expenses of the partnership. The partnership itself does not pay a tax. However, you have to report your share of the partnership's net income on Schedule E (Supplemental Income and Loss) on your personal tax return Form 1040.

As a sole proprietor or partner in a business you have to pay estimated federal income tax and self-employment tax. Form 1040ES is used to make quarterly estimated tax payments on or before April 15, June 15, September 15, and January 15. However, if you are incorporated, the last estimated tax payment is due December 15 instead of January 15.

Records supporting entries on a federal tax return should be kept until the statute of limitations (ordinarily three years after the return is due) expires. Records relating to depreciable property should be retained for as long as they are useful in determining the cost basis of the original or replacement property.

The records must be accurate and complete and must clearly establish income, deductions, tax credits, employee information, and anything else specified by federal, state, and local regulations.

29

CORPORATE TAXES

As a corporation, you are required to file Form 1120 and are subject to corporate income taxes. Corporate tax rates are higher than personal tax rates. For example, most companies are taxed at the marginal federal tax rate of 34 percent while most individuals are taxed at the marginal tax rate of 28 percent.

The corporate tax return is due on the fifteenth of the third month subsequent to the company's year-end. A company may elect a calendar year-end December 31 or a fiscal year-end (any other one-year period). For example, if there is a December 31 year-end, the tax return must be filed by March 15.

The federal corporate income tax rate is graduated as follows:

Taxable Income	Tax Rate
$50,000 or less	15%
50,001–$75,000	25%
Over $75,000	34%

Although corporate income tax returns are filed at the end of the taxable year, quarterly tax payments are required if the company has to pay estimated tax of $40 or more.

If you have a regular corporation, the net loss from the business is unavailable to offset your nonbusiness income. However, you can carryback the net loss three years and then carry it forward 15 years to reduce profitability.

If you are incorporated (except as an S Corporation, described in Chapter 30), you are subject to double taxation. The net income of the corporation is taxed (Form

1120), and then you are taxed again on your personal tax return (Form 1040) on the salary or dividends received from the corporation.

A capital gain or loss results from the sale of a capital asset (e.g., equity or debt investment, real estate). The gain or loss is the difference between the selling price and cost and is subject to tax.

Seventy percent of the dividends received by a company from a taxable domestic corporation are exempt from taxation.

Fringe benefits paid to employees are tax deductible. Examples are pension plan contributions and health insurance premiums. Further, food and entertainment-related employee benefits are fully deductible.

Business meal and entertainment expenses are 80 percent deductible. However, transportation to and from the restaurant is 100 percent deductible.

Promotional items intended for public distribution, such as samples, are fully deductible; deductions for business gifts are limited to $25 per individual recipient.

Your company may elect to expense immediately *up to* $10,000 of certain types of personal property instead of capitalizing and depreciating them.

A charitable contribution is *generally* deductible up to 10 percent of taxable income without taking into account the contribution. A charitable contribution in excess of the limitation may be carried forward five years.

If you have slow-moving or excess inventory, consider donating it to a charity to obtain a tax deduction. You can deduct the cost of the item plus one-half the difference betwen the cost and market value, not to exceed 200 percent of the cost. For example, if an item costs $1,500 and sells for $2,500, you are eligible for a charitable deduction of $2,000 ($1,500 + .50($1,000)). Some charitable organizations you may contact in this regard who will supply the necessary tax documentation are The National Association for the Exchange of Industrial Resources (309-343-0704) and Gifts in Kind America (703-836-2121).

Other deductible expenses include depreciation, interest, professional fees, casualty and theft losses, and bad debts. Nondeductible expenses include fines and penalties.

You can request from the Internal Revenue Service (IRS) a free guide to tax rules and regulations. Publication number 910 (IRS's Guide to Free Tax Services) will provide helpful information on business tax issues. Publication number 334 is a tax guide for small businesses. Also request a business tax kit (IRS 454) that includes relevant business tax information. A toll free telephone number is 1-800-424-3676.

State, cities, towns, and counties may impose their own taxes. The taxes may include income taxes, payroll taxes, unincorporated business taxes, personal property taxes, and real estate taxes. Make sure to contact the appropriate office of your respective state and locality for information.

30

SUBCHAPTER S CORPORATION

A Subchapter S Corporation is a business structure option available only to the small business. It is simple to form and operate. S Corporation combines the limited liability of a corporation and the single-taxing advantage of a sole proprietorship or partnership. Thus, it avoids double taxation!

You can elect to organize as an S Corporation by filing Form 2553 with the Internal Revenue Service on or before the fifteenth day of the third month of a year the election is to take effect. Most S Corporations report on a calendar year rather than a noncalendar fiscal year, since each individual shareholder is taxed on that basis. Thus, the deadline for the election is March 15.

An S Corporation files an information tax return on Form 1120S and attaches a Schedule K-1 for each stockholder, showing his or her portion of taxable income or loss for the year. This is similar to the partnership return, which reports and assigns income to each partner. Thus, there is no tax to the S Corporation; rather the individual reports his or her share of the S Corporation's net income on his or her personal tax return Form 1040, Schedule E, Part II (Income or Loss from Partnerships and S Corporations). The stockholder is able to offset any business losses against his or her personal income. Hence, the protection of incorporation is coupled with tax savings.

If you wish to incorporate as a Subchapter S Corporation, you must meet the following requirements:
• All stockholders must agree to S Corporation status.
• Each stockholder must be an individual.
• There cannot be more than 10 stockholders.
• A certain percentage of the company's income must

be from actual business operations and not from passive sources.
- No stockholder can be a nonresident alien.
- There must only be one class of outstanding stock.

An S Corporation can have any amount of assets or net income. There is no restriction on size.

Once an S Corporation reverses its election, it cannot again decide to be taxed in this manner for five years.

31

PAYROLL RECORDKEEPING AND TAXES

You should obtain an employer's identification (I.D.) number for tax purposes by filing a Form SS-4 with your local IRS office. The employer I.D. number is used on filed tax returns and is different from your social security number.

An employer, regardless of the number of employees, must maintain all records pertaining to payroll taxes (income tax withholding, social security, unemployment tax) for at least four years after the tax becomes due or is paid, whichever is later.

A new employee must fill out his or her appropriate exemptions and sign Form W-4 (Employee's Withholding Allowance Certificate). You then withhold income tax based on the IRS's withholding tables. If the employee for some reason does not prepare a W-4, treat him or her as a single person with no withholding exemptions. Make sure to tell your employees to prepare a new certificate if their status changes (e.g., there is an increase in the number of their dependents). This new certificate must be filed prior to December 1 of the next year.

On or before February 28, you have to provide employees, the IRS, and state and local tax agencies with copies of Form W-2 (Wage and Tax Statement) listing salary earned and taxes withheld for the last calendar year.

If an employee in your business receives tips of $20 or more in a month, you must report these tips for tax purposes on or before the tenth of the following month.

You have to deduct social security taxes from the employee's salary, and you must match the employee's contribution. In addition, you must pay your own social security tax. You must file form W-3 with the Social Security Administration.

Form 941 is used to remit withholding taxes and social security deductions to the IRS. Form 941 must filed by the last day of the month following the end of the quarter. For example, Form 941 for the first quarter of the year (January 1 to March 1) must be filed by April 30. You must also deposit the withholding and social security deductions in a separate account. This is accomplished with Form 501 (Federal Tax Deposits, Withheld Income, and FICA taxes). This form, along with the remittances, is sent to a bank authorized to accept tax deposits. In an emergency, the IRS will accept deposits filed with Special Form 3244 at the local office.

Unemployment tax is paid to both the state and the federal government. The IRS gives a partial credit for unemployment taxes paid to the state. You must first register with your state Bureau of Labor; you will then receive an identification number so that your deposits will be credited to your account. Your experience rate will partly determine how much unemployment tax you must pay; the rate will change depending on how many employees you hire and fire. For example, if you terminate a lot of employees, your unemployment tax rate will increase because of the higher demand placed on the state's unemployment fund. Your particular state will inform you how and when to deposit unemployment taxes.

The federal unemployment tax (FUTA) is less than the state rate. One month subsequent to your taxable year-end, you must file Form 940 with the IRS to show how you computed the unemployment tax. If the tax is under $100, you may remit the amount directly with Form 940. If the amount exceeds $100, you should use a Special Deposit Card 508 (Federal Unemployment Tax Deposit) and pay the tax to an authorized bank. Usually you must have three full-time employees before your tax will exceed $100.

If you hire individuals to perform services as independent contractors, you must file an annual information return (Form 1099) to report payments totaling $600 or more made to any individual in the course of trade or business during the calendar year. Be sure your records list the name, address, and social security number of every independent contractor you employ, along with pertinent dates and the amounts paid each person. Each payment you make should be supported by an invoice submitted by the contractor.

32

SALES AND
EXCISE TAXES

Sales taxes are levied by many states and cities at varying rates. When you contact the respective sales tax departments for instructions on how to register as a collector of sales taxes, you will be told which buyers are exempt from sales tax, which forms to file, and how to deposit sales tax monies you collect with the state and/or local governmental agency.

Most states provide specific exemptions for certain classes of merchandise or particular groups of customers. Service businesses are often exempted altogether. You can devise a control to identify tax-exempt sales from taxable sales; then you can deduct tax-exempt sales from total sales when you file your sales tax returns each month. If you fail to collect taxes that should have been collected, you can be held liable for the full amount of uncollected tax.

In many states, wholesalers or manufacturers may not sell to you at wholesale prices unless you can show them your sales tax permit or number, also called a seller's permit. You usually have to sign a tax card for their files. The seller's permit allows you to buy tangible personal property for resale without having to pay sales tax to the vendor. In order to get a seller's permit, contact the sales and use department of the state. (You should also remit sales tax to this office.) A fee may be assessed to obtain the permit. You may also have to give a security deposit in the event you fail to remit appropriate sales tax. If the security deposit in your state is very high, try to arrange an installment payout.

When your customers buy from you, add the tax (where applicable) to their purchases. You then submit it to the appropriate agency, with the forms designed for the purpose.

When conducting business across state lines, you are not required to collect taxes for any states other than those in which you maintain offices or stores.

The Internal Revenue Service collects federal excise tax. Currently, excise tax must be paid by manufacturers of coal, truck parts, tractors, firearms, tires and lubricating oils, and telephone services, and for the use of international air travel facilities. Computed quarterly on Form 720, the tax can be sent with the form if the total tax is under $100; otherwise, the tax must be paid to an authorized bank along with IRS Deposit Card 504.

33

MARKETING RESEARCH AND PLANNING

Marketing research is the process by which marketing data are obtained, recorded, and evaluated. It identifies potential consumers and how to meet their needs and considers pricing strategy, product introduction, and the best means of advertising. Marketing research aids in segmenting your market into specific groups of consumers and in differentiating your product.

Marketing research answers numerous questions, including the following:

- What is the degree of competition?
- Who are the potential customers by income, age, and geographical location?
- Are you offering the product at the right time in the right place at the right price?

The major areas of marketing research are:

1. *Internal Information.* This is based on your own records, such as sales, cash receipts, aging of accounts receivable, and complaints. Carefully note your customer profile. What makes your customers tick? Customer addresses are revealing because they tell you where your customers live and their approximate income.

2. *Secondary Research.* This involves obtaining information already compiled by another source, such as private companies, government agencies, books, or periodicals. The cost of obtaining this information is minimal; often the information is free. An example of a source that provides already-prepared

marketing research reports is Mediamark Research, 341 Madison Avenue, New York, N.Y. 10017.

3. *Primary Research.* This involves either doing the research yourself or retaining an experienced researcher to do it for you. The two types of primary research are exploratory and specific. *Exploratory research* is directed at trying to define the problem and is usually accomplished by detailed interviews with a restricted number of interviewees. It is an open-ended approach. *Specific research* is used when the problem has already been defined. It concentrates on solving the problem. Its sample size is significantly larger than that of exploratory research, and the interviews are complete and structured.

You may engage marketing research firms to evaluate which new products to introduce and to provide advice about consumer and industrial research. You can then find out whether your new product idea is feasible.

The steps in the marketing research process follow:

- Identifying and defining the problem (e.g., identifying the customer base).
- Ascertaining whether marketing research will help.
- Specifying objectives.
- Enumerating information to be collected (e.g., sex, age, and employment of potential customers).
- Picking the research instrument (e.g., mail interview, personal interview).
- Deciding on a sampling method (e.g., random sampling).
- Determining a sample size from the population.
- Collecting the information.
- Tabulating and appraising the data.
- Formulating conclusions (e.g., customer base, best product line).
- Taking desired action.

A plan is needed for the optimal marketing of your product or service to assure success. This marketing plan should be documented with supporting facts and should

97

be updated as needed. Information in the marketing plan includes segment, size of market, market share, distribution channels, competition, pricing alternatives, product costs, legal issues, geographic locations, production constraints, growth trends, customer profile, and industry trends.

A marketing plan achieves the following objectives:

- It clarifies where resources should be allocated.
- It aids in communicating to current and prospective employees what must be done.
- It serves as a guide to actions and steps to be taken.
- It helps you to take advantage of opportunities.
- It identifies problems.
- It fosters control.

Determine what product image you want to portray. Do you want to be seen as a retailer of high-priced, high quality goods or services, or as a retailer of low-priced merchandise? Once you have decided upon an image, your actions must then be consistent with that image in such areas as pricing, merchandise selection, packaging, advertising, mode of sale, and dress.

The Ps and Qs of selling that you should practice are these: Plan your sales effort, and be personal, pleasant, persistent, and patient. You should conform to high standards and be proud of your product.

You may need to give discounts and allowances to wholesalers, retailers, and others to induce them to carry the line.

You should use marketing effectiveness measures to gauge your marketing success. This includes determining product profitability by product line, class of customer, size of customer, average order size, age group, industry segment, geographic area, channel of distribution, and type of marketing effort. Potential sales problems and growth opportunities should be noted, and you should compare objectives and actual performance. New product evaluation should be done in terms of risk and return.

34

PRODUCT INTRODUCTION

A key area for the survival and success of any new business is the introduction of new products and/or services; this area is especially important in a highly competitive environment. New product introduction involves not only the idea or product itself but also forecasting the cost of developing and manufacturing the product, its profitability, target sector, life expectancy, and selling price and then bringing that idea as a product to the store shelves. A smaller company has one advantage over a larger one—it can do customized work.

The product life cycle runs from introduction to growth to maturity to decline. Of course, life cycles vary among products, however, generally speaking, old products eventually lose their appeal and may become unprofitable.

Outside professionals can help you as you work to bring a new product to the marketplace. Patent attorneys and agents can assist in finding patents and preparing applications to obtain a patent. Packaging designers can aid in properly designing the packaging and containers for your product. Advertising agencies may be retained to handle promotional efforts. You can hire management and marketing consultants who may aid in appraising potential sales, formulating a selling price, analyzing the competition, developing a marketing program, and examining the cost and availability of raw material sources. Industrial engineers can assist in designing the new product for greatest efficiency, best appearance, and lowest cost. They can also iron out any product defects.

Advantages of new product introduction include:

- Increasing sales and profitability.
- Reducing overall overhead by using idle facilities.
- Strengthening existing products. This is so because the new product increases the overall size of the company's product line.
- Penetrating new markets and distribution channels.

In deciding on whether to introduce new products and what kinds to introduce, you should ask yourself the following questions:

- How much is your budget for new product introduction?
- How many units can you sell and at what price?
- What is the cost of the product?
- How profitable will the product be?
- What are the expected return on investment, break-even point, and payback period?
- What is the expected turnover rate?
- Are there any potential product liability problems and warranty difficulties? What is the ease and safety of use, servicing, and packaging?
- Are there stringent government regulations?
- Who is the competition and what are its strengths?
- What is the product's seasonality?
- Does the product fit the company profile?
- How will the product be promoted?
- Who is your market (e.g., consumer, industry, government)? What is the size of the market?
- What is the probability of the product's success?
- Will product demand be limited geographically?
- What is the expected life cycle of the product?
- Can you maintain product quality control?
- How long will it take to market the product?
- What are the available distribution channels?
- Will the new product fit into the existing product line easily?
- Does the product have a synergistic effect upon other products?
- Are warehouse facilities adequate?
- What is the quality of the salespeople?
- Are production workers skilled?

For answers to new-product development questions that come up, you may contact the Association for the Advancement of Invention and Innovation, Suite 605, 1735 Jefferson Davis Highway, Arlington, Virginia 22202.

35

ADVERTISING

The objectives of advertising are to reflect a company's positive image, generate sales, and make consumers aware of the product line and/or services. The amount you spend on advertising should at least equal the revenue to be derived from it. Before planning an ad campaign, however, you should be able to answer these questions: What is your budget, degree of competition, and the expected benefits from the advertising? What is the percent of advertising to sales common in your industry?

Advertising effectiveness can be determined by looking at the sales and profit before, during, and after promotion. Were there any competitive reactions? Response to ads will increase when you provide a business reply card; coupons and games may generate a good response rate. A code number should appear on reply cards so you can identify how the respondent found out about the product.

In evaluating the market, you have to determine who will buy the product or service (e.g., age group, income level). There are different strategies for segmenting the market that may be used, including creative, media, and positioning. In creative, you change the words in different ads depending upon who will read them. In media, you select the best medium to reach the target audience (e.g., television or radio). In positioning, you aim your product at those most likely to be motivated to buy it. A market may be segmented in terms of sex, social class, age, occupation, education, income, marital status, family size, ethnic group, geographic location, subculture, percentage of working women, and health.

Types of advertising include:
1. *Commodity.* This is advertising designed to promote a specific brand, usually an unestablished one.
2. *Mass Advertising.* This is designed to reach a cross-section of the population.
3. *Advertising by Class of Customer.* This kind of advertising is directed at the type of person who will buy the product (e.g., sports enthusiasts).
4. *Institutional Advertising.* This type of advertising gives a message about the company and may not promote a specific product.

Your advertisement should include all necessary information about the product, including what it is, what it does, when to use it, and how to use it. Emphasize why it is better than competitive products.

The positioning of the advertisement on the page, its size, its layout, and its content will have an effect on consumers' minds. Further, the advertisement should be timely (e.g., tied to a season, holiday, or local event). If you use an advertising agency, select one that has experience with your product or services. You may obtain a free ad in a publication if you have a new product or service that may influence the general readership.

In selecting a particular media source, you should consider:
1. *Cost.* Is it within your available funding?
2. *Type and Number of Audience.* Does it reach your desired audience?
3. *Frequency of Ad.* How often will the ad be run?
4. *Consistency.* Is the ad consistent in satisfying the desired marketing mix (e.g., product, price, distribution)?
5. *Demographics.* What are the demographics of the advertising?

Different types of media include: (1) directories (e.g., Yellow Pages); (2) print (e.g., newspapers, magazines); (3) direct mail; (4) outdoor (e.g., billboards); (5) broadcasts (e.g., television, radio); (6) specialty items (e.g., pens); and (7) movie screen.

Compare the various media sources to select which is best for your particular product or service. For example, while newspaper ads are cheaper than television ads, they provide limited demographic selectivity. Put advertisements in different media in different weeks to see which generate the biggest increase in business.

When negotiating with a media source, ask about seasonal discounts, special discounts (e.g., volume ads), barter arrangements, professional assistance, the availability of lowered rates for standby status (in the event available space or time still exists just prior to a television show), and per inquiry charge, by which you pay for only those sales generated directly from the ad.

36

SALES FORCE

Selecting a sales staff involves the following steps: (1) reviewing application forms; (2) checking references; (3) interviewing; and (4) observing performance on a sample run in the field.

In negotiating a compensation package for salespeople, keep in mind that: (1) compensation should include salary plus commission; (2) compensation should include fringe benefits; and (3) compensation should be competitive.

Personal selling involves face-to-face dealing. The advantages of personal selling are that it permits repeated attempts to get the sale; it offers quick feedback on the sale or on related information (e.g., product quality, complaints); it provides flexibility in adjusting sales terms; and it allows specific identification of the customer. The drawback of personal selling is its high cost.

Salespeople should be kept current on all product information, including manufacturing and marketing aspects. They must be thoroughly familiar with the product line in order to instill confidence in consumers. Salespeople may do much more than just taking the order; they may push other products, get overall customer feedback (e.g., complaints), and show how to use the product. Salespeople should communicate complaints they receive on the road about the product or service to responsible parties, such as manufacturing and marketing managers. There must be cooperation among all members of the organization in handling such complaints.

If your salespeople are on fixed salaries, your selling costs will drop as volume increases. You should have specific policies regarding expense reimbursements:

What is reimbursable and how much? As part of internal control, you should audit salesperson expenses.

Measures for evaluating the performance of salespeople include: (1) sales volume and dollar sales; (2) comparison of actual sales to budgeted sales; (3) profit generated; (4) number of new accounts; (5) call frequency; (6) percent of sales made to the number of calls (closing ratio); and (7) market penetration.

The plan for compensating and recognizing salesperson efforts should maximize the company's financial interest and motivate salespeople. The plan should preferably provide for: a minimum salary; commission based on a graduated profit; bonus for meeting the sales quota; payment to salespeople only after collection is received; higher commission rate for original business than for repeat sales; higher commission rate for a more difficult territory; some flexibility in setting the selling price depending on competitive factors and customer dealings; and higher commission rate for success in pushing slow-moving items. Sales quotas should be based on past experience and amended in light of the current environment.

A customer profile should be developed (e.g., type of business, previous orders, buying history, or personality traits).

If you are a manufacturer, you may decide to use as a sales representative an independent agent who sells the products of several companies on a commission basis. Such representatives are managed by in-house sales managers. Sales representatives may be found in trade magazines and industry publications, including directories, and by recommendations from others. Examples of directories are *The Directory of Manufacturers Agents* (McGraw-Hill) and The Manufacturers and Agents National Association's *Directory of Members*.

A sales representative should *not* carry items that are competitive with yours but may handle items related in terms of type, quality, and price. He or she usually sells to specific areas or industry groups. You should initially limit the sales territory for sales representatives until you can evaluate their commitment and performance. Since the sales representative is experienced, seriously consider any advice he or she may offer. You will have to give the agent exclusive rights to your product in a particular territory. Sales representatives should preferably be used for high-dollar volume items. Of course, while the agent obtains the order, you ship and bill the store directly.

Using a sales representative may be advisable if you have a limited product line, want to accomplish product acceptability quickly, or have a long sales training period. Advantages of using a sales agent are that you do not have to pay a fixed salary plus fringe benefits, paying a commission only if there is a sale; you may gain greater expertise and contacts in a specific territory or market, particularly if the market is thin, the territory is widely dispersed, and there is insufficient volume to support a salesperson. Disadvantages of using a sales agent are that a higher commission rate is typically required; you have less control over the individual and his or her selling methods; agents usually are less familiar with your product and give only a part-time selling effort to it; agents have less company loyalty and may "steal" your customers when the contract expires.

A new business may find hiring a sales representative attractive because it provides immediate service without the time and costs involved in hiring and training a sales force. However, if there is a high sales volume, the sales representative may not be able to give the service an in-house sales force is capable of.

37

PRICING

Pricing must be in line with the style, quality, and service of the product. If your price is too low, the sales volume will be high, but the revenue may be inadequate to cover costs. If your prices are too high, sales volume will be low, and you may not be able to cover operating costs. As you set prices, you should consider market conditions, competitors' prices and proximity, costs, return experience, income of clientele, and sales volume. You should test the market to see the effect on product demand of altering the product's prices; the price quoted for future delivery may be different than that for immediate delivery since market conditions may change.

The selling price of an item affects its profitability. Pricing should be taken into account particularly in the following situations:
- Introduction of a new product. Since no established market yet exists, costs will be the key ingredient in establishing a selling price.
- Product life cycle.
- Market penetration.
- Inflationary or recessionary periods.
- Reaction to price changes of competitors.
  The price charged affects the following:
- Profitability of the item.
- Company image. A high price implies in the minds of buyers a higher quality item.
- How long it will take to recover the investment.
- Market attractiveness.
  Factors in establishing a selling price are:
- *Rate of sales.* A fast-selling item can have a lower markup, since it brings in money via higher volume,

while a slow-moving item may require a higher markup to compensate for lower volume.

- *Manufacturer's fixed price.*
- *Use of leaders.* A leader is a good typically offered at a lower selling price than competition in order to increase store traffic. It might be sold at a slight profit or even at a loss just to attract business. A loss leader is sold below cost. A good leader is one used daily and bought frequently.
- *Life cycle of item.* A novelty item has a good markup until competition sets in; a fashionable good generates a good markup until the fashion is over. There may be drastic markdowns at the end of the season.
- *Type of item.* A staple item typically has a lower markup and does not benefit from promotion. It is sold because it offers value and price. Lower-priced lines sell more quickly and have lower handling costs. A staple gives value to consumers. If low-priced items are found satisfactory, the same consumer may become a user of the popular and high-priced lines.

The different basic pricing approaches for a new product include:

1. *Competitive pricing.* Here, the price is based on what the competition is charging. For consumers to switch to your product or service, you must offer something unique (e.g., better service, higher quality, reliability, more congenial staff).
2. *A low price (penetration).* This strategy enables you to enter a new, competitive market by selling at a low price. The hope is that the low price will result in greater volume. Unfortunately, a low price may imply low quality. Once consumers get used to your product, you may raise the price.
3. *A high price (skimming).* This strategy may be used for a new product having no competition. It can also be used when you want to give the product an image of quality. As competition enters, you can begin to lower the price.

Three basic pricing policies are:

1. *Single price.* One price is charged to all buyers irrespective of quantity ordered or timing. This policy is easier and consistent in administration. However, large volume buyers will be turned off because they expect a price reduction.
2. *Negotiable (variable) price.* This enables you to modify the price as need be (e.g., competitive reactions, "tough volume," high-volume order, promotional program). The drawbacks are perceived price discrimination, causing possible resentment from those paying a higher price, excessive price reduction by salespeople eager to get the sale; and possible violation of law.
3. *Nonvariable price.* The same price is offered under the same conditions; a different price applies under different conditions. This strategy is easily administered and is fair to all buyers within a specified category; all salespeople must stick to the same price so there is no room for possible abuse. In this way, you keep control over pricing and avoid legal exposure.

Often a selling price is based directly on the cost of the item. A markup may be added to cost based on what is typical in the industry. For example, if cost is $10 and a 50 percent markup on cost is desired, the selling price will be:

Cost	$10
Markup (50 percent × $10)	5
Selling price	$15

The markup may vary depending on the type of product, demand, competition, and marketing factors. For example, if you introduce a new product that is in heavy demand and faces no competition, you may assign a higher markup. On the other hand, you may assign a lower markup to a product with heavy competition.

The retailer may decide to mark down the selling price to make it more attractive for consumer purchase, especially when the item is slow-moving or becoming obsolete. Markdowns may also stimulate sales volume.

If you introduce a new product or service but consumers will not pay the price you charge, you may make a minimal profit or in fact face a loss. In this case, your options are to:
- Reduce the price. This will lower profit.
- Eliminate the product.
- Lower costs, possibly by cutting corners.
- Emphasize product differentiation from competitors' products by promoting higher quality, better service, and quick delivery.

A discount may be offered. The different kinds of discount policies are:

1. *Quantity.* A discount is given, sometimes graduated, with an increased order size.
2. *Promotional.* A discount is offered to buyers to promote the product or service.
3. *Trade.* A discount is offered in the ordinary course of business within the distribution network. For example, a manufacturer may offer a discount to a retailer.

Pricing should take into account the elasticity of product demand. A company can increase the selling price of an item having inelastic demand (e.g., pharmaceutical items) because a change in price will not have much adverse effect on sales volume. However, if price is increased on an item with elastic product demand (e.g., fur coats), sales volume may fall off significantly.

You can evaluate the demand for a product based on a change in price by surveying customer reactions to different possible prices, and comparing the product's price to a similar or replacement product.

A business is prohibited from price discrimination as per the Robinson-Patman Act of 1936, which prohibits a business from selling a product or service at different prices to two or more competing customers engaged in interstate commerce if the activities result in injury to competition. However, a business is permitted to sell at different prices if cost differences exist.

38

PACKAGING

Packaging should provide protection during rough transit and should ensure that the product will be delivered to the consumer in good condition. Interior reinforcement and cushioning may be required for fragile items, and boxes containing delicate goods should be marked "Fragile." The packaging should withstand climate and temperature problems and minimize delivery costs.

Do not use extravagant, costly packaging such as unnecessary padding and wrapping. Labeling on the package should be informative and distinctive and have all the information required by law.

The packaging cost should be low relative to the selling price of the item. If the packaging is for the ultimate consumer, the packaging should be consistent with the style of the merchandise.

39

TRADE SHOWS

Attending a trade show may enable you to obtain a significant increase in business. Attend those trade shows having the highest probability of increasing sales. Some publications listing forthcoming trade shows are *Exhibits Schedule* (Bill Communications) and *Trade Show Convention Guide* (Budd Publications).

Before finally deciding on a trade show that initially looks good, ask for literature about that show and examine such things as who attends and their job titles, the expected number of attendees, the markets served, and location of booths.

After selecting a trade show to attend and designing your exhibit, try to do the following before the show:

- Inform the media (e.g., trade magazines), customers, and sales representatives that you will be there.
- Prepare posters and brochures.
- Pack and ship merchandise before the show starts.

Advantages of attending a trade show are that you can:

- Promote your company's image.
- Sell your goods.
- Demonstrate and distribute information about products. You may see if new products are of interest to attendees (a sort of market testing). Get attendees' names and addresses.
- Meet with customers, suppliers, sales representatives, and competitors.
- Develop a new distribution channel.

40

MANAGING THE BUSINESS

One of your first tasks in managing your business is to select a name for it. If you are establishing an unincorporated entity, you may use the owner's name so there is no requirement to file a certificate of name. However, if you select a name other than that of the owner, a certificate of the business name must be filed with the county clerk. If you plan to establish an incorporated business, you, or more likely your attorney, must file with the state in which the business is located.

Most businesses are started because someone creates a unique product or way of marketing a product. Even though this first notion is important, long-term planning is essential concerning products, additional financing, capital expansion, marketing, and advertising. This can be difficult for the average entrepreneur, because many entrepreneurs are not great problem solvers. They tend to put off dealing with potential problems until a crisis arises and they are confronted with them.

One reason a new business may turn out to be a disaster is that for the first time the entrepreneur must be a true leader and not a doer. He or she must now manage people and work with them to make this business work!

The owner must be well-rounded. He or she is responsible for supervising employees, planning the direction of the firm, developing new products, controlling costs, and promoting the business.

Work has to be performed with quality workmanship and materials; there can be no cutting corners if the entrepreneur wants to succeed. The entrepreneur's creativity and dedication are vital to the success of the business.

Office Management. An office manager may be needed to monitor office procedures, assign work, oversee performance and proper use of supplies, prepare and circulate important memos, and assure that office equipment is properly used.

Labor is the most expensive part of running an office. Therefore, increasing labor efficiency may lower costs. Time and motion studies may be conducted to ensure that worker operations are cost-effective and time-efficient; each office operation should yield a cost-benefit. Duplication and delays in activities should be avoided. Part-time employees may be hired for short-term, unskilled duties; for example, high school students may work after school at a minimum wage.

Cost savings may be achieved in several ways. Workers should turn off lights and electronically-driven machines when they leave their desks at lunch or for other long periods. Obsolete forms may be used as scratch paper. Check with private long distance telephone companies to see if they offer discount rates. You can do the following to save on mailing costs:
- Determine the price and delivery time of less costly ways to mail catalogs.
- Instead of using stamped, self-addressed envelopes for replies, you may use business reply cards and envelopes that allow you to pay only for those actually returned.
  To save time in handling, do the following:
- Use addressing machines.
- Use envelope openers.
- Use postage scales.
- Use tying and bundling machines.
- Use sorting racks and tables to expedite sorting and dispatching mail to various departments.

Do expenses appear reasonable? You may look at the trend in the relationship of cost of supplies to total cost, cost of supplies to sales, and telephone expense to sales.

The documents, stationery, and forms should simplify

your company's activities. The instructions on the forms should be clear as to purpose and procedure. Computerized programs may be used to prepare forms suitable for your unique needs. You can prepare the computerized forms as need be with modification.

In the office, planning, execution, and coordination activities occur. Many customers and clients have their initial contact with the business at the office; therefore, it should give a good impression. The physical layout and size of the office depend on the type of business, but they should promote efficiency. The office space should contain provision for a reception room, storage, and vaults. A conference room may also be needed. There should be restrooms, a coatroom, and a coffee machine. You need good lighting to reduce workers' eyestrain and fatigue.

Before buying office equipment, try to get a demonstration of it. Also, find out if the employee who will use the equipment is comfortable with it. Will the purchase of lower cost, used equipment suffice? If your needs for equipment are heavy only in certain times during the year, you may be better off leasing than buying. The desks and chairs should be comfortable. Desks should have sufficient drawer space and compartments, racks for stationery and accessories, and letter and filing trays.

You should have preventive maintenance done for office equipment and take out service contracts for such machinery. Keep a control record for each piece of equipment, including serial number, manufacturer, model, cost, date of purchase, and location. If repairs to a piece of equipment run 20 percent or more of its cost, the equipment should probably be replaced.

Most offices need a photocopying machine. You may also need facsimile (FAX) transmission to transmit letters, drawings, and typed or printed material electronically over telephone lines.

41

INSURANCE

You will require insurance to protect against various business risks, including casualty loss (fire, hurricane), illness or death of key personnel, employee strike, and product liability. You should identify the possible risks, appraise the probability of the loss occurring, the dollar amount of potential loss, what dollar insurance you feel comfortable with, the premium required on the policy, how much of the risk you are willing to accept yourself, and the term of the insurance policy.

You should practice risk prevention and/or reduction by having a sprinkler system, fire alarm, and safety equipment. You may also transfer risk of damage to another party to reduce the need for insurance; for example, you may subcontract the production of your product or rendering of services to pass on risks (e.g., employee injury, water damage). You may decide to lease property, in which case the lessor maintains the insurance.

It is preferable to use one agent to handle your insurance needs, since responsibility then rests with one individual and you will at the same time lower overall cost. When you have a package (comprehensive) insurance policy, inquire how the premiums are computed and obtain the price breakdown for each type of coverage. Make sure to keep careful records of your insurance policies, premiums, and recoveries. Further, a periodic appraisal may be necessary to determine fair market values of your insurables; for example, it may be better to insure your inventory separately so that the insurance rate may be adjusted on a periodic basis to tie into its changing carrying value. Review insurance coverage regularly so that you do not pay excessive premiums on property values that have declined!

In deciding which insurer to select, consider the following:

1. *Financial health of insurance company.* Will the insurance company be around and have the financial resources to pay out a huge settlement?
2. *Insurance services needed.* You may need a specialized type of insurance that is better provided by an insurance company specializing in your industry.
3. *Cost.* You should choose the insurer who charges the least for the coverage and deductible involved. In looking at cost, consider the total premiums to be paid (initially as well as later ones) and any dividends to be received. *Beware:* If the cost is unrealistically low, perhaps claim settlement may be a problem and/or services may be inadequate.
4. *Ability to modify coverage.* Is the insurance company flexible in tailoring the policy to meet your particular needs? Will the insurance company allow you to insert desired provisions?

In setting premiums, the insurance company will classify the business according to the degree of risk. Businesses that are not very high-risk include children's clothing stores and beauty salons. Moderate-risk businesses include restaurants, auto sales, and grocery stores. High-risk businesses include gas stations and liquor and jewelry stores.

Notify the insurance carrier as soon as a loss occurs. Make sure you can document the loss for insurance reimbursement purposes by having careful accounting records, a death certificate, or inventory listings.

If you are in a high-crime area and are unable to obtain insurance privately, you may be able to obtain government insurance through the Fair Access to Insurance Requirements Plan. Rates vary depending upon geographic location, area crime statistics, and gross receipts. You can determine if your state uses this plan and if you qualify by contacting the state insurance commission.

Be watchful of overlapping coverage in insurance policies, which causes a higher-than-necessary cost and may result in problems in case of a loss if each insurance company denies basic liability and wants to pay only the excess not covered by the other company.

The various types of insurance coverage are:

Liability Insurance. You are legally liable for negligence that results in accidents and mishaps causing injury to customers, employees, or any other party somewhat connected to your business. An example is an individual who falls and is injured because of a defect in the floor in your store.

Surety Bond. A surety bond, usually taken out by construction contractors, guarantees that you are honest and capable of performing the contractual obligation. To obtain the bond, you will need to put up collateral. If you do not properly perform, the surety bond company will pay the customer the resulting damages. This bond helps the small contractor compete with large well-known contractors because it guarantees the job to the customer.

Product Liability. Product liability exists for damages caused by the company's products or services to customers. Note that the coverage may be limited to only a certain type of product.

Fidelity Bonds. The bonding company performs a check on employee honesty. There are different types of fidelity bonds: Individual bonds cover each employee separately, while schedule bonds list the names or positions of those to be covered. Blanket bonds cover the whole work force. Bonds are continuous unless canceled by either party.

Key Man Insurance. If an owner, partner, or major employee becomes disabled or dies, you are covered for the resulting business losses. If the key-man insurance is taken because it is required by a lender as protection for the loan, the insurance cost is *not* tax deductible.

Property Insurance. Property insurance provides reimbursement for loss to business property. Business property includes real property (e.g., building) and personal property (e.g., office equipment, machinery, inventory). Property coverage includes comprehensive, theft, fire, sprinkler leakage, flood, hail and windstorm, vandalism, inland marine, and glass. Each of these is discussed below.

Comprehensive Property Insurance. This policy basically covers all risks except those specifically excluded in the policy. Some advantages of this policy are that it offers lower cost than if the coverage were purchased in separate policies, it avoids duplications in coverage with separate policies, and it enables you to obtain settlement more easily by avoiding the conflict possible in individual policies. Typically, comprehensive policies exclude coverage for automobiles, accounting records, cash, and machinery.

Theft Insurance. While comprehensive property insurance may include some types of crime, other types are excluded and may be separately covered in theft insurance, including employee theft, defalcation, embezzlement, and off-premises robbery. Crime insurance includes burglary and robbery.

Fire Insurance. A standard fire insurance policy covers fire and lightning. A special policy is needed for additional risks such as coverage for theft and property protection after a fire.

Sprinkler Leakage. This covers losses due to leakage of a fire protection water sprinkler system.

Hail and Windstorm. This is usually covered as part of the comprehensive, all-risk property insurance.

Vandalism. This is typically part of a comprehensive policy.

Flood. A separate policy is needed to cover flood damage.

Inland Marine. This floater policy is directed toward special types of retail businesses, including jewelers, furriers, and launderers. This type of property is very vulnerable to loss.

Glass Insurance. Glass insurance provides reimbursement for breakage in the store's glass windows.

Credit Insurance. Credit insurance includes credit life

and commercial credit. Credit life is designed for retail businesses selling on credit and guarantees that if a customer dies, his or her debt will be paid off. Commercial credit reimburses you if customers default on their balances.

FAIR Plan. If your small business is located in a crime-ridden area vulnerable to significant vandalism and riot, you may not be able to get private insurance; if you can, the fee may be exorbitant. You may, however, qualify for the Fair Access to Insurance Requirements (FAIR) plan sponsored by the U.S. Department of Housing and Urban Development.

Transportation Insurance. Transportation insurance provides coverage for your goods while they are being transported. This coverage provides peace of mind since common carriers are usually not liable for catastrophes such as flood or acts of God. An inland transit policy covers losses from a land shipment not insured by the common carrier's policy; a blanket motor cargo policy is for those who ship by truck.

Automobile Liability Coverage. In addition to being responsible for accidents caused by your own vehicles in the course of business, you may be legally liable for accidents caused by vehicles of others acting on your company's behalf (e.g., employees, suppliers). Coverage usually includes collision, fire, theft, and liability. Note exclusions such as breakage to glass. You can lower the premium cost by having a higher deductible and joining a safe-driver program.

General Liability Coverage. General liability coverage typically includes reimbursement for losses resulting from bodily injury or from damage to property of others, medical costs associated with the accident, and legal and court-related costs. Check the policy for exclusions, such as damages that result from blasting operations or that are related to nuclear energy. Check the liability limitations of the policy; the limit may be per person or per accident. For example, an automobile liability insurance policy may limit you to $300,000 per person injured or to a total of $1,000,000 per accident.

Umbrella Policy. An umbrella policy covers unusually large losses that exceed your basic coverage. An example is additional coverage for accidents caused on company premises exceeding basic coverage of, for example, $2 million. The umbrella policy may cover an additional $3 million in losses. For a relatively low cost, you may be protected against severe losses.

Workers' Compensation Insurance. Workers' compensation insurance covers the employer if the employee is injured on the job. An employer is required by law to give employees a safe place to work and safe tools and equipment and to warn employees properly about possible dangers they face in the performance of their jobs. An employer who fails to take any of these actions may be legally liable. The employer's liability is less if the employee was careless or if another employee was responsible for the injury.

Business Interruption Insurance. If your business is shut down because of a catastrophe, you will suffer lost earnings. In addition, you will have to continue paying business expenses. This insurance reimburses you for both lost earnings and ongoing expenses.

Profit and Commission Insurance. This insurance reimburses you for lost profits or commissions due to destruction of the related merchandise.

Valuable Papers Insurance. Valuable papers insurance covers the business against damages resulting from the destruction of important documents.

Malpractice. Malpractice insurance may be taken out by professionals including accountants, attorneys, insurance agents, engineers, and architects.

Rent Insurance. This reimburses you in the event your tenant fails to pay his or her rent.

Health and Life Insurance. Health and life insurance cover illness or death to the owner and/or employees. Coverage usually includes basic health insurance, major medical insurance, dental insurance, and life insurance. Health and medical insurance typically cover basic hospitalization, laboratory tests and include major medical plans and disability plans. Life insurance provides payment to the employee's family if the employee dies. You may be able to use life insurance annuities to provide employee pension benefits. Group insurance coverage will result in lower rates than if the policies were taken out individually.

42

IMPORTANT RECORDS

There are many important records needed to keep track of what is going on in your business. These records include sales records, service records, purchase records, and equipment records. In addition, you will need to keep financial records (e.g., cash receipts, cash payments), payroll records, insurance records, and personnel files. These are discussed in other Keys.

Safeguard documents and records against loss by placing duplicates in different locations. Then, if one set is destroyed, you have a backup copy somewhere else.

Sales records can be used to measure the efficiency of individual selling departments or sales staff. The records can reveal which department is making the best profit, which department operates on the closest margin, which salespeople are generating the most sales, and how their individual sales records compare to their wages and to the sales performance of the other salespeople in the department.

The sales record can be obtained by several methods, including cash register totals, daily sales slips totals, or individual records of sales kept by sales staff. Department sales can be obtained by using departmental keys on the cash register, by using separate cash registers for each department, or by totaling the sales slips of each department. Sales records of each salesperson can be obtained by requiring the salesperson to identify himself or herself on each sales slip or by using an identification code when ringing up sales in the cash register.

Service records maintain a file on merchandise that has been returned by customers for service. If the item is under warranty, the repair cost will have to be borne by the merchant or the manufacturer; if the repair is not covered by warranty, the cost will be paid by the customer. The purpose of the service record is to ensure efficient handling of transactions, prevent loss of goods, and ensure payment by the customer or the manufacturer. A complete record should be maintained for each service call, whether warrantied or not, including work performed. Repair charges should be uniform to facilitate bookkeeping and ensure fair treatment of customers. Obtain suggested repair rates from the manufacturer for common repair problems.

Purchase records maintain control of credit purchases and ensure that payments are made on time. A daily invoice file should be kept for each month. Invoices should be filed under the day they will become due, making it easy to check the file on a daily basis to see what invoices need to be paid. Once paid, each invoice should be filed alphabetically and marked with the check number and date of payment.

Keep equipment records for all equipment owned by the business, and include relevant information such as the purchase date, description, cost of the equipment, fair market value (if known), down payment, monthly payment, balance, and accumulated depreciation. This information is useful for internal control, recordkeeping, insurance, and replacement.

43

COMPUTERIZING THE SMALL BUSINESS

A computer will greatly increase the productivity of the business by lowering recordkeeping costs and providing timely and accurate information for decision making. Initially, a computer consultant may be retained to teach the owner and staff how to use the hardware and software.

Before purchasing a personal computer system, the small business owner should consider the needs of the business in terms of volume, types of computer applications, and kinds of software needed. What are the company's information requirements, paper flow, and expected growth? Do not buy a system that you will outgrow in a few years! However, a possible alternative for first-time users might be a service bureau.

Computers are useful in many areas, including processing business transactions, recordkeeping, preparing financial statements and tax returns, inventory recordkeeping and control, purchasing, preparing status reports for customers and salespeople, preparing special reports such as aging customer accounts, financial analysis, storing information such as documents and correspondence, generating electronic mail, scheduling, calculating, and linking files.

Accounting software exists to do all the recordkeeping of the business, including recording transactions in the journal and maintaining a ledger. The software has different modules such as cash, accounts receivable, inventory, accounts payable, payroll, and fixed assets.

Spreadsheet software is also available for the preparation of forecasts, budgets, "what-if" analysis involving alternative assumptions (e.g., the effect of product line strategies on profitability or of change in sales on profitability), cash flow analysis, and breakdown of expenses by category.

A database management system package is an organized collection of readily accessible related information that may be used on a recurring basis. Examples are records of customers, inventory, and employees. The database program allows you to enter, manipulate, retrieve, display, extract, select, sort, edit, and index data.

Tax preparation and planning software, including software to maintain payroll records, are widely available, as are financial analysis packages, such as programs for cash management, anticipating the consequence of a policy change (e.g., increasing selling price), or investing funds.

Also useful are decision software programs that place you in different business scenarios in which you make strategic business decisions. The programs evaluate your decisions, instruct you on the merits of your decision, and make suggestions as to what other alternatives you should have considered.

You can use a word-processing program with a mail-merge feature that individually addresses and changes text in form letters. The program also prepares mailing labels and sorts by ZIP code, allowing you to save money on presorting bulk mailings.

Desk-top software may be used as an appointment calendar, as a record of time spent with particular accounts or projects, or as a notepad or mail and telephone directory. Other uses include telephone dialing, card filing, and preparing custom forms.

Marketing research programs can be used to design your research tool and to analyze the data and interpret the results. Computers also assist in maintaining customer lists, finding new customers, and performing media research.

There are graphic packages that put numeric information into such graphic forms as charts, diagrams, and signs.

Planning and scheduling software exists to assign work to employees and to keep a record of the customers to be serviced and the type of tasks to be performed.

Time and billing software can be used to keep track of hours spent on an account by type of function performed so you can bill the customer based on an hourly rate.

You should select your software first, since it will help determine the hardware required. Since it is usually best to get a package that will operate on most computers, IBM-compatible software is the best choice.

Prepackaged, general-purpose software should be considered before industry-specific software or custom programming. The prepackaged software will typically do the job at significantly lower cost. But be cautious about bargain packages, since the software applications may be limited or the program may be of poor quality, lacking flexibility, or accompanied by unclear manuals.

Prepare a list of the hardware requirements of each software package you intend to buy, including necessary and recommended: memory, extended memory, monitor, operating system, disks, speed, and peripherals. Based on the list, put together a package of hardware that will adequately run the software you have selected. Make sure the hardware can accommodate the total number of devices. You will need to buy additional units as your needs grow.

Once the software and hardware have been purchased, it is time to install and implement the system. The implementation process is typically time-consuming and problem-filled. The best way to implement various software and applications is in modules, giving several weeks to the learning and implementation of each. For example, with an accounting package such as BPI Accounting, accounts receivable may be learned and implemented in the first month, payroll in the second, and inventory in the third. Make sure to involve the employees who will be using the system early in the process. Run a manual backup for several weeks as insurance because the computerized system may initially result in errors and failures. Obtain an insurance policy covering the new system, including provision for a replacement; you might also take out a service contract. Have a second backup of data stored on disk in case the first one is destroyed for some reason (e.g., human error, computer malfunction). The two disks should be kept in different locations.

Once a system has been implemented, it should be reviewed for conformity to performance standards, such as the speed and accuracy of reports.

If data should be restricted for use by only certain employees, proper access controls such as passwords are needed.

You may make use of telecommunications to access on-line databases to obtain business and financial information, as well as to place orders for goods. There is a vast number of databases available, including investment information, vendor information, and tax and banking data. (For a comprehensive guide, refer to the New American Library's *The Computer Phone Book: Directory of On-line Systems.*)

If computers at different locations are linked to a central computer, electronic mail, allowing a typed message in one office to appear on another computer, may be used.

44

THE RECRUITMENT PROCESS

The steps in recruiting personnel are identifying your staffing requirements, formulating job specifications and minimum employment standards, interviewing, and hiring. In identifying personnel requirements, you should know what your business is going to accomplish and segregate that objective into tasks. You then determine what type of person will best perform each task and how many hours will be required to accomplish it. Prepare a list of individual positions, needed qualifications, and when the position will begin.

You should prepare a detailed job description for each position, listing what the job entails, name of supervisor, name of position, why the person is needed, salary range, previous experience and education required, travel requirements, working hours, and overtime required.

It is always good to promote from within for morale purposes; it also saves money in recruiting. You can try to recruit from competitors talented employees who have experience and contacts; this will hurt your competition. You may also obtain secret information that will help your business.

The hiring process involves the following steps:

1. *Screening applicants*. This involves looking over applicant resumes and selecting those who meet your minimum standards to interview.
2. *Interviewing*. The structure and questions for the interview should be prepared beforehand and a rating sheet used for major categories such as personality, knowledge, and communication skills. Make sure you are not interrupted during the interview.

Have the applicant fill out an application form before the interview and review it prior to the meeting to know what areas to concentrate on.

3. *Making an offer.* Check references and supporting documentation before making a job offer. Try to give the offer in person or on the telephone rather than by letter, since personal contact is best. Offer the applicant a salary about 10 percent below what you think he or she will accept, assuming it is a fair figure. You can always negotiate later. Emphasize other positive aspects about the job besides salary, such as fringe benefits, working environment, and promotion opportunities.

According to equal employment opportunity laws, you cannot discriminate against an applicant on the basis of race, religion, or sex.

Recruitment efforts may be in the following forms:

1. *Word-of-mouth.* This method is easy and is the least costly. Employees and professional associates may recommend suitable candidates. A disadvantage is that you will not reach many potential candidates.

2. *Placement agencies.* You will pay the agency only if you hire a candidate. However, the fee may be significant. The candidates have already been screened for appropriateness for your job.

3. *Advertising.* You may advertise in newspapers, journals, and trade publications. You may use a blind ad with only a box number in order not to identify the name of your business. However, blind ads will attract fewer responses than open ones because applicants like to know who they are dealing with. An advantage of advertising is the ability to quickly locate candidates; the response rate is typically high enough to find a suitable candidate.

4. *College campuses.* When recruiting on college campuses, emphasize responsibility, experience, and rapid advancement. College recruitment does not involve a placement fee.

5. *Professional associations.* Some professional asso-

ciations permit you to place recruitment ads in their publications. This is advantageous because you are targeting a desired audience.

You may use a temporary agency for temporary help. Advantages are that they offer flexibility, can be used on a need basis, and impose no cost for fringe benefits. Disadvantages are a higher hourly rate, a lack of employee long-term commitment, and reduced employee experience in the business.

45

MANAGEMENT OF EMPLOYEES

The most important resource you have is your capable employee staff. A congenial and professional relationship should exist between you and your employees, and you should meet with your staff on a regular basis. Good employees should be rewarded and recognized financially and with promotions.

You have to pay your employees fair wages. If compensation is too low, the employee's morale will be bad and they may leave. If the salaries are too high, you are rendered less competitive and lose money you should not lose. Typical salaries and fringe benefits in the industry may be learned from professional organizations and associations, industrial organizations, local chambers of commerce, the U.S. Bureau of Labor Statistics, and executive recruiters. Bonuses should be based on employee job performance and/or the profitability of the company. Semi-annual reviews are a good idea. In looking at the compensation package, you have to consider not only salary but also fringe benefits (e.g., health plan, retirement plan). Most fringe benefit payments are tax deductible. Also important are job security, working conditions and hours, employment terms (e.g., sick leave, vacation time), status (e.g., job title), and treating employees with dignity and respect. Generally, an employee is given two weeks vacation after one year and three weeks thereafter.

In determining a salary rate, consider these factors:
- Salary should be based on worker productivity and performance.
- Higher salary should go with more experience and additional years of service.

- Wage rates should be adjusted depending on demand/supply factors.
- A person who is overqualified for a job should be moved to a more reasonable position.

It is in your interest to try to motivate employees because then they will be more productive and will achieve corporate goals to the maximum extent. A lack of motivation will result in job friction, poor quality work, turnover, absenteeism, and lateness.

You can minimize disciplinary problems by ensuring that all employees know company rules and the reasons for them. There should be goal congruence built on trust and understanding. Rules and guidelines regarding job expectations, absenteeism, lateness, theft, and drunkenness should be reasonable and clearly stated. The punishment for breaking a rule must be communicated. Preferably, the rules and punishments should be developed in a participative manner between the employer and employees. In extenuating circumstances, you may bend the rules; however, avoid favoritism. Be open to employee suggestions regarding employment terms.

There are many labor laws governing such areas as minimum wages, maximum hours, overtime pay, and job discrimination, so consult with a knowledgeable professional (e.g., labor attorney, personnel officer).

Before terminating an employee for cause, give at least one warning. If an employee must be terminated, do it at the end of the working day in a meeting that is free of interruptions and carefully explain the reason for your action. Remember to be tactful because of the effect of the firing and the employee's reaction on other employees. Preferably, severance pay and unemployment insurance should be given. If you have confidence in the employee, try to find him or her another job.

Before hiring temporary employees, consider paying overtime to current employees. Temporary employees may be hired when there is a rush order, seasonal demand, employee illness, or if the workload suddenly increases. Some drawbacks exist, however, in that the temporary employees do not know your company's operation and involve a higher cost because of the extra compensation that must be paid to the placement agency.

You may contact a temporary employment agency which has already hired experienced employees, the employees may already be covered by insurance from the employment agency. Inform the service of your needs and provide full information about the job, length of time help is required, qualifications and skills required, nature of your business, and office equipment to be operated.

When the temporary employee reports for work, you should:
- Be realistic in expectations.
- Inform your permanent workers.
- Provide for proper supervision to explain what to do.
- Be patient, since it will take time for the temporary employee to get to know the ropes.
- Plan the wordload.
- Ready the equipment.

46

OPENING A FRANCHISE

A franchise is a license to sell a product or service within a certain territory. Many types of franchise businesses exist, including restaurants, travel agencies, and recreation services; examples include Dunkin' Donuts, McDonalds, and Baskin-Robbins. There are ads for franchises in daily newspapers such as *The New York Times* and *The Wall Street Journal*.

With a franchise, the owner can run a small business but have the advantages of a big business, using the franchisor's reputable name, product, or service. The probability of success with a franchise is higher than if you start from scratch.

Before entering into a franchise agreement, inquire about the franchisor at the Better Business Bureau, local bank, and Chamber of Commerce. Also, consider how many competing franchises already exist.

The initial franchise fee, covering training, marketing assistance, product research, and recordkeeping, may be as low as $5,000 and as high as several million dollars, depending on the reputation of the franchisor. (You will also receive a support system and discount prices on supplies.) Further, there are typically royalty payments based on sales and a fee for advertising and promotion. The total cost can be significant, resulting in lower profit margins compared to those of independently owned businesses.

In deciding upon a particular type of franchise, select an industry that you are comfortable with. Are you professionally and personally right for that type of franchise? You should consider product life cycle, growth rate, product demand, and demographics. Select a mature or growing industry, not a declining one.

Contact the franchisor you are interested in directly or deal through a franchise broker. You may contact the International Franchising Association, 1350 New York Avenue, N.W., Washington, D.C. 20005. This association puts together deals and offers advice. A good book listing the names, addresses, and all needed information about franchisors is *Franchise Opportunities Handbook* (Washington, D.C.: U.S. Government Printing Office). Other useful books are *Directory of Franchising Organizations* (Pilot Books, 347 Fifth Avenue, New York, N.Y. 10016) and *Franchise Annual* (InfoPress, 736 Center Street, Lewiston, N.Y. 10942).

Before entering into a contract, obtain preliminary information from the franchisor. The Federal Trade Commission Franchise Rule requires all franchisors to furnish you with the names and addresses of a minimum of ten franchisees closest in proximity to you. Obtain from these franchisees their opinions of the franchisor. Further, under the Federal Trade Commission rules, the franchisor or franchise broker must provide the prospective franchisee with a disclosure statement containing particulars about the franchisor at the earliest of the following three dates:

- Ten days before payment is to be made.
- Ten days prior to executing the contract.
- At the first personal meeting between the franchisee and franchisor.

The Federal Trade Commission law also requires the following:

- The franchisor must give the prospective franchisee an earnings claim document if the franchisor makes a statement as to the return the buyer may expect. This earnings claim document must be updated every 90 days for actual income statistics. The franchisor has civil liability for any misstatements.
- The franchisor must give the franchisee a copy of the agreement at least five days before the contract is to be executed.

The disclosure document should contain the following information:

- Name and address of franchisor.
- Criminal and civil actions against the franchisor.
- Background of chief executives.
- Franchisor's financial statements for the prior three years.
- Previous statistics of franchises, including the number of operations, number terminated by either party, and renewals refused.
- Payment terms, including initial and annual fees.
- Description of product line and market.
- Life of franchise.
- Termination and cancellation clauses.
- Restrictions placed on franchisee, including territorial restrictions and products to be sold.
- Duties of franchisee.
- Nature and cost of training.
- Financing arrangements including interest rate and collateral.

The ownership agreement with the franchise varies; the franchisee may or may not own the property. The percentage of sales the franchisee must remit to the franchisor may also vary.

Consult with your attorney and accountant in appraising all aspects of the franchise arrangement.

47

SERVICE BUSINESS

A service business has as its major source of revenue the fees charged for services rendered to consumers; typical service businesses include specialized repair and maintenance services, home and health services, beauty parlors, dry cleaning establishments, leisure facilities, and financial advice firms (e.g., brokerages). The success of the business depends on the owner's and employees' skills. The risk is matching your characteristics and skills with the right service business. There is typically an absence of significant investment in fixed assets.

Make sure to do quality work at reasonable prices. Further, always *guarantee* your work to instill consumer confidence.

When starting a service business, make an announcement (e.g., in a local newspaper) and offer an incentive to motivate customers to contract for your services. Examples are a free initial office consultation or a free oil change. Make sure to be included in the yellow pages of the telephone book.

In a service business, personal recommendations are the best source of customers. Always be honest and open, and avoid using high-pressure tactics.

Check what federal and local regulations affect the business including minimum wage, fair employment, safety and hazard, and pension rights regulations.

48

THE RETAIL STORE

A small retail store cannot compete with chain retailers in terms of variety, price, and cost control. The small retailer should concentrate on offering unique goods, an attractive shopping environment, and personal service. You can specialize to give the business a niche; customers going to small retail stores may be looking for merchandise or services not usually found in a chain store. Cater to customer tastes and have convenient hours; express appreciation to your customers for their business. Any customer complaints should be handled immediately, and appropriate credit given. Good payment terms should be given to regular customers for high-priced items. Be honest with customers such as by recommending a lower-priced item that will do the job. Perhaps you can offer a longer warranty period than competitors and repair services for a greater range of problems.

Selectively seek out potential customers, perhaps by getting a list of recent homebuyers in the community. Computers can generate a list of customer names and addresses by age, sex, income, geographic area, and housing. Also, you may give a contribution to a community drive to get recognition and promote future business.

Sales staff should be sincere, well-informed, and properly dressed. The customer should always be given the benefit of the doubt. If there is a special sale, it should be genuine.

The store should be easy to enter or leave when competitive stores exist (e.g., three gas stations in close proximity). Customers do not like to wait in cars. The middle of the block may be easier to access and may also have a lower rental.

The retail store may be a specialty shop. If there is competition in the immediate vicinity, offer better selection, carry higher-priced or lower-priced product lines depending on the situation, and have more attractive displays.

Stock advertised and private brands. There is typically a higher profit margin on brand items.

A discount store typically deals in one product line or several related product lines and emphasizes high turnover items. You can lower costs by having a self-service store.

Signs and show windows give some clue as to the prices and types of merchandise or services available. The window displays should be attractive and informative.

Staple items should be put in the rear of the store (except when on sale) and impulse items should be placed in the front of the store. Customers will be attracted to the impulse items on their way to buy the staples.

Try to balance the departments in the store against one another. Space in one department should not be disproportionate to others unless that department is expected to generate significant sales volume. Place departments selling bulky items with low sales volume in the rear of the store; place departments with high volume items in the front of the store.

Send reminders for the next scheduled appointment for services such as car maintenance and carpet cleaning.

There are tricks of the trade in certain types of retail stores. For example, in a clothing store, the fitting rooms should be private, lighted well, and mirrored. In a restaurant, patrons want cleanliness and privacy.

49

THE WHOLESALER

The wholesaler acts as an intermediary between manufacturers and retailers. The majority of wholesale firms purchase materials in large quantities, warehouse them, break them down into small shipments, and distribute them. Wholesalers must respond quickly and accurately to retail orders to keep loyalty.

The wholesaler should know what to stock, where to cut costs, how to price merchandise, how to advertise and market, what product lines and fads are developing, what geographic territory to serve, how to use credit wisely, what records to keep, and how to monitor excessive and shortage situations of goods. The wholesaler can provide valuable information to retailers on running their businesses in such areas as pricing, selling, kind and quantity of inventory to maintain, selecting equipment, financing, and deciding upon a suitable location. An aggressive wholesaler may provide financial assistance by giving the retailer initial stock on extended credit terms.

Inventory management is crucial. High turnover is important in controlling the obsolescence of goods; slow moving items have to be identified.

Inventory control may be maintained by (1) observation, (2) periodic stock count, and (3) perpetual record-keeping. Ideally, the inventory control system measures the actual amount of stock on hand of each item, its value, amount sold, and amount purchased. Since the observation method relies on judgment and memory, it is not a good method to use. The stock count method is a periodic count providing an indicator of the rate of movement and the quantity on hand. It provides a record of experience with the item; however, it is susceptible to possible error. A perpetual inventory record is a daily record of inventory balances, including purchases, receipts, sales, and returns. Physical inventory is compared to book inventory, and any discrepancies are noted. Good inventory control will help to reduce turnover, minimize thefts, and eliminate slow-moving merchandise.

Profit and loss should be determined by customer, commodity, brand, department, and territory. Larger order sizes reduce credit, delivery, and selling costs.

A successful wholesaler provides unique, superior, and profitable items. The wholesaler must sell goods to retailers at reasonable prices so the retailers can resell them at competitive prices. The wholesaler may take back goods the retailer cannot sell.

A good layout is needed in the warehouse to be cost-effective. Receiving, stocking, order picking, order assembly, and shipping should be organized. In stocking, there should be economies of storage, replenishment, locating, and retrieving.

You must know your costs by item and by hour. What are the industry norms for the costs? Are your costs high, low, or about right? Why? You have to monitor your costs on a regular basis.

It is important to have sound territorial management. If you overextend, your costs will be excessive in relation to the volume of orders you obtain. If you do not extend enough, you will lose sales you could have had. Profitability should be determined by a territory, considering selling and delivery costs. Before entering a new territory, evaluate the degree of competition and determine your ability to effectively compete.

An effective cost control system is needed, including minimizing transportation costs. Perhaps you can share distribution centers with another wholesaler. It may be cheaper to contract delivery outside than to buy and use your own trucks.

The wholesaler should try to keep the retailer from bankruptcy if there are financial problems by extending the repayment period or easing credit terms.

Your mailing list should not go to customers who buy

from your salespeople. In this way, you the wholesaler can offer price incentives to your best customers. Also, do not mail price sheets to customers who are in direct competition with your good customers. Further, after two mailings within a reasonable time period, those customers who do not respond should be deleted from the mailing list. Finally, mail order wholesaling may be used to obtain sales outside of your usual delivery area; in these cases, delivery costs should be prepaid by the customer.

Computers should be used in order processing, record keeping, and inventory maintenance in order to speed up the flow at low cost with minimal errors.

50

MAIL-ORDER BUSINESS

Many consumers buy from catalogs to save time and cost. The catalogs allow consumers to buy many products in a leisurely atmosphere. To determine items available from suppliers that you may wish to include in your mail order catalog, refer to the *Mail Order Business Directory* published by B. Klein and Company. The Direct Marketing Association, 6 East 43rd Street, New York, N.Y. 10017, has literature on mail order sales. The mail-order business provides opportunities for good profits, but there are risks of losses and even bankruptcy.

You have to decide whether the type of products you wish to sell are suitable for mail-order sales. If the products spoil easily, mail order may not be suitable. What is the survivability in physical terms? The products must be sold in sufficient quantity to justify the costs of selling them; printing and mailing catalogs are costly.

The mail-order business can deal only with a manufacturer who will deliver the merchandise on time. Purchases should be made direct from the manufacturer to avoid the middleman's profit; product selection must be made carefully to ensure demand, quality, and ample supply. The product line must be flexible to meet competitive pressures.

Is the market a general population or a segment thereof? Is the market national, regional, or local? Try to get the manufacturer to give you exclusive territorial rights.

You will achieve greater sales if you offer merchandise on installment terms, providing a discount to customers who make immediate payment in full.

Give customers the option of faster delivery at an extra

charge. In any event, try to send out the merchandise quickly. If there is a delay, notify your customer and closely watch the order; in such a case, the customer should be given the option of cancelling the order. (According to Federal Trade Commission rules, a customer may cancel any order not received through the mail within 30 days of the order). If you do not fill the order, customers may complain to the FTC or to the state's attorney general, prompting an investigation.

Damaged goods should be replaced immediately. If a dispute arises, the customer is always right; give an immediate refund if the customer requests it.

It is against Federal Trade Commission rules to make misleading "free" offers, to substitute one product for another without permission, to fail to give refunds, and to follow questionable collection practices. You should make sure you properly advertise what the product is in order to minimize returns. Returns cause bad will, along with extra handling and postage charges.

In direct mail, you send advertisements to consumers who are likely to order the product. The mailing list includes those who have bought from you before. Mailing lists are often purchased; you may obtain a list of mailing list houses from the Small Business Administration. You may rent a mailing list through a broker, with an additional charge each time you use it. The broker's commission is typically 20 percent of the fee charged to renters of the list. Sometimes, competitors may exchange mailing lists to avoid the broker's commission; you may also be able to use public information, such as a telephone directory.

The mail-order package typically includes a sales letter, circular, order form, and business reply envelope. And 800 telephone number should be included. To find the best mailing list, you may initially send out sample mailings from several different mailing lists and see which one gives you the best response.

Mail-order ads may be placed in newspapers and magazines that your target audience is likely to read. Try to convince buyers that your product is better in price, quality, or status than the competition's. The more information contained in the ad, the greater the likelihood of making a sale. Your ad should have a full description of the merchandise, along with an order blank. CAUTION: You are legally liable for any false or misleading information about the merchandise. If you employ an advertising agency, make sure it is not retained by your major competitors.

Check for possible problems with your product with the Federal Trade Commission, Food and Drug Administration, Better Business Bureau, or postal authorities. Consult an attorney about possible product liability problems; and take out proper insurance.

Booklets describing postal rates, regulations, and requirements affecting the mail-order business may be obtained from the Customer Programs Division, U.S. Postal Service, Washington, D.C. 20260. If you presort the mail by ZIP codes in bundles, you may reduce the postage rate. Your postmaster must approve business-reply cards and envelopes. You need a permit, for which an annual fee is charged, for bulk rates. Postage meters can be used to save time and reduce rates. You may want to determine if you will save both time and money by using a private mailing service, such as United Parcel Service.

QUESTIONS AND ANSWERS

1. What are some basic questions an entrepreneur should ask himself or herself?

Some questions an entrepreneur should ask himself or herself are: Am I willing to work long hours? Do I get along well with people? Can I pay bills on time? Do I like this type of business? Do I know all the risks I will face? Am I a good salesperson? Can I make decisions? Am I organized? How am I in an emergency? Do I know all the costs I will incur? Am I a good planner?

2. What are some make-or-break requirements for running a small business?

In running a small business, do the following: (1) Be objective and honest; (2) Recognize the strengths and weaknesses of the business; (3) Keep it simple and focused; (4) Concentrate on areas of profitability; (5) Provide quality goods and services at reasonable prices; (6) Satisfy the customers' needs; (7) Motivate employees; (7) Have good accounting records and internal controls; (8) Watch the cash; (9) Understand your business; (10) Plan properly; (11) Avoid excessive risks.

3. What are some typical questions a bank asks about a small business loan proposal?

Typical questions asked by a bank are: (1) Has the owner committed a significant amount of his or her own money? (2) Will there be enough cash flow to cover debts? (3) Is the business overly dependent on customers or suppliers? (4) Can the business survive a financial crisis? (5) What is the value of the assets used as collateral?

4. What sections should be included in a marketing plan?

A marketing plan contains the following sections:

- *Company organization.* This section points out how each major segment of the organization will be involved with the proposal.
- *Background and description of business.* This details project information and what is expected to be achieved.
- *Statement of the problem.* Highlights any potential problems facing the project so possible solutions may be offered.
- *Budget.* States the cost of the project to see if there is a favorable cost benefit/relationship. Does the company have the financial resources to succeed?
- *Executive summary.* This contains an overview of the project and objectives. It identifies what is to be done and the financial resources required.
- *Financial plans and projections.* Makes financial projections for sales, profit, assets, and cash flows.
- *Enumeration of opportunities.* Discusses potential opportunities that may exist with the project.
- *Analysis and evaluation of situation.* Enumerates the particulars of the project, including targeted market, legal issues, competitive factors, and product demand.
- *Time schedule.* Specifies the time it will take to complete each task of the project.
- *Structure of the project.* Specifies the organization of the project and notes the background of project leaders.
- *Marketing strategy.* This enumerates how the market will be reached and at what cost.
- *Implementation of strategy.* Discusses how the strategy will be initiated and identifies success, failure, and problem areas.

5. What are some ways you can turn unprofitable products into profitable ones?

You can turn unprofitable products into profitable ones by doing the following:

- Change the price, either upward or downward. A price reduction may increase sales volume; a price increase may occur without causing a material fall off in business. An increase in price of a necessity item (e.g., medicine) will not necessarily cause a drop in volume. If quality improves, consumers generally do not mind paying a higher price.
- Make the product line simpler, perhaps by reducing the number of qualities and sizes. Simplification results in lowering distribution costs and permits concentrated selling and advertising efforts and lower production costs.
- Modify advertising based on sales generated.
- Repackage the product. A change in packaging may improve sales volume and lower storage, handling, and delivery costs.

6. What are sources for new products?

Some sources for new product ideas are:

- A product on which you can imprint someone's name, such as a pen.
- Available products that you may distribute, as listed in the Thomas Register of Manufacturers.
- Currently existing products that are doing well. However, you must make sure yours is somewhat different to avoid patent infringement.
- Products available from major corporations, who may license them to small businesses.
- A product whose patent has expired after 17 years, that is in the public domain, and that therefore may be manufactured by anyone.
- Government-owned patents that may be licensed as commercial properties. These are listed in Patent Abstracts Bibliography, available from the National Technical Information Service, U.S. Department of Commerce, Springfield, Virginia 22151.

The Official Gazette of the U.S. Patent office lists all patents granted and those available for sale or licensing. You can also contact license brokers who represent companies having products they want to license for another's use.

Another possibility is successful foreign products not currently available in the United States. You may act as a representative of the foreign country in the United States.

You might also attend an inventor exhibit or trade show. Inventors are looking for someone to produce their product. At a trade show you may uncover interesting possibilities.

The business opportunity section of financial publications (e.g., *The Wall Street Journal*) lists possible ventures; you can also contact Small Business Investment Companies (SBICs) and investment bankers who may be aware of new products by a new venture.

7. What are some ways to reduce costs?

Costs may be reduced as follows: (1) Eliminate small, unprofitable orders; (2) Assess a handling charge for small orders; (3) Reduce services offered (e.g., repairs); (4) Lower clerical costs; (5) Establish minimum order sizes; and (6) Substitute mail-order solicitation for personal calls.

8. In marketing a new product, what should be considered?

In marketing a new product, take into account: (1) Consumer attributes (e.g., occupation, age, location, sex, income level); (2) Uniqueness of product; (3) Competitiveness of the product; (4) Pricing and quality of the product; and (5) Distribution channels.

9. What can you do to lower your insurance costs?

Insurance costs may be reduced by doing the following:
• Obtain competitive bids from insurance carriers.
• Have a higher deductible. A deductible is typically a specified dollar amount, but it may be stated as a percentage or a time period.
• Determine if you are getting what you are paying for. Are premiums worth the protection you are getting?

- Package insurance policies to get a lower overall rate than if each policy were purchased separately.
- Ensure there is no duplicate coverage for the same item.
- Periodically review the adequacy of insurance coverage.
- Install a prevention system to lower premiums.
- Review the policy carefully, looking for unneeded items for possible deletion.
- Determine your track record in receiving insurance reimbursements.

10. What personal characteristics should your sales people have?

The personal characteristics of good salespeople include: (1) reliability; (2) analytical ability; (3) ability to make quick and correct decisions; (4) intelligence; (5) good oral communication; (6) outgoing personality; (7) professional demeanor and appearance; (8) willingness to travel; (9) ability to take customer questions and possible abuse; (10) convincing demeanor, and (11) knowledge of industry, company, and competition.

11. What are some ways to motivate your employees?

Employee motivators include: (1) Good salaries, fringe benefits, and working conditions; (2) Open lines of communication; (3) Promotion opportunities; (4) Recognition and praise for jobs well done; (5) Employer flexibility; (6) Opportunities for input; (7) Feeling part of a team; (8) Opportunities for independence and thinking; (9) Immediate feedback; and (10) Opportunities for initiative and innovation.

12. In looking over a franchise agreement, what questions should you ask?

The following questions are relevant when dealing with the franchisor: (1) Are the contruction and maintenance standard guidelines specified by the franchisor reasonable? (2) Are you obligated to buy from the franchisor equipment, inventory, and trucks? (3) What are you getting for the franchise fees? Is the annual fee fixed, based on a percentage of sales, or some combination? (4) What insurance coverage is required? (5) What quota restrictions exist? (6) What employment terms, such as wages, fringe benefits, and uniforms, are required? (7) How may ownership be transferred? (8) Who sets the prices, procedures, and hours of operation? (9) What are the limitations on the sources of supply? (10) What contribution, if any, do you have to make to national advertising? Are there any rules regarding local advertising? Must you participate in promotions? (11) How are disputes settled? Typically, arbitration is provided for.

13. How may your business violate antitrust laws?

Antitrust violations may occur when two or more competitors agree to split the markets, fix prices, or require a customer to buy another item with the item sold. A business can quote different prices to different consumers only if proper economic justification exists.

GLOSSARY

Acceleration clause a clause in a credit or loan agreement that states if the borrower does not meet the payment schedule, all remaining payments may become immediately due and payable at once at the demand of the creditor or lender.

Accommodation a loan without interest, collateral, or other consideration. An example might be a loan between members of the family or friends in order to start a business.

Account a record of the relationship and transactions between a business and another party (e.g., customer). The account balance is what is owed at the end of a reporting period.

Action a legal proceeding initiated by the business against another party such as for the nonpayment of a customer's account balance.

Adjustment 1. Changing an account balance because of some happening or occurrence, such as a product defect. 2. In insurance, the settlement of a claim.

Advance 1. Money given to an employee before it is earned, such as an advance against salary. 2. Payment received from customers in advance for work, goods, or services. 3. Money given by a banker to a borrower; in advance, usually short term and in the form of an overdraft.

After-tax cash flow net cash flow (cash revenue less cash expenses) after taxes have been subtracted. It is the cash flow generated from operations.

Allowance the reduction in price or increase in quantity of a good or service that the seller gives the buyer. Allowance may be given in special sale, damage, shrinkage, and spoilage situations.

All risk/all peril a feature in an insurance policy that covers all risks/all perils unless specifically excluded by the policy.

Amortized loan a loan that is paid off in periodic equal installments and includes varying portions of principal and interest during its term.

Appreciation increase in value of an asset such as property.

Approval sale a sale which is not finalized until the merchandise is accepted by the buyer. Title will pass only when approval is given or when the goods are retained by the buyer for a reasonable time period or that period specified in the agreement.

As is a term for secondhand or damaged goods sold without either an express or implied warranty by the seller. The buyer is warned to inspect the items carefully since the burden of determining their condition falls on him or her.

Balloon clause a provision in an installment sales agreement stating that the final payment by the customer will be substantially larger than all other payments.

Bank reconciliation a term used when reconciling the differences between the bank statement and the checkbook balance. The checkbook balance must be the same as the bank balance at the end of the period. Reconciling differences relate to (1) items shown on the checkbook but not on the bank statement (e.g., outstanding checks) and (2) items shown on the bank statement but not on the checkbook (e.g., bank service charges).

Bargain basement a physical location in a large retail store where merchandise can be bought at significant discounts.

Bill of sale a receipt of money paid by the buyer to the seller.

Billing cycle the time period between periodic billings for merchandise or services rendered, typically one month. It could also be the periodic mailing of statements within a month to distribute the work load efficiently.

Blanket rate the same rate paid for transportation charges for a delivery of merchandise to buyers within a given geographic area.

Boilerplate standard language found in contracts and agreements.

Bounced check a check that has been returned for insufficient funds.

Cash and carry a requirement that a customer must pay a retail store in cash for a good or service and either take immediate delivery now or arrange for delivery (at a charge).

Cash before delivery a requirement by a seller that the buyer pay for goods before delivery. A discount may be given for immediate payment. The seller may do this when it feels a risky or questionable buyer is involved.

Cash budget a budget for cash planning and control that presents anticipated cash inflow and cash outflow for a specified time period. The cash budget helps the owner keep cash balances in reasonable relationship to needs. It assists in avoiding idle cash and possible cash shortages. The cash budget shows beginning cash, cash receipts, cash payments, and ending cash.

Casualty insurance insurance that protects a business against property loss and damage.

Closed corporation a corporation in which shares are held by a few individuals, typically family members or management of the company. These shares are not available to the public.

Collateral property that must be pledged as security for a loan. If the borrower defaults, the lender can usually seize the collateral.

Commencement of coverage the date upon which insurance protection starts. Prior to that time, the risk of loss belongs to the owner of the business.

Common stock a security which represents ownership in a company.

Company car an auto owned by the business but available to an employee for use.

Compensating balance the balance a borrower must maintain on deposit in a bank account, representing a given percentage of the loan. No interest is earned on this balance, which increases the effective interest rate on the loan.

Concession 1. A reduction in the price a seller charges

as an incentive for sales. 2. Any deviation from normal terms or previous conditions. 3. Permission, usually in the form of a lease, to conduct a particular type of business in a specific area or place.

Contract of sale a written agreement between seller and buyer in which the purchaser agrees to buy specified merchandise or services and the seller agrees to sell them upon the terms of the agreement.

Corporation a form of business organized as a separate legal entity with ownership evidenced by shares of capital stock.

Credit a loan extended to a business or individual payable at a later date.

Credit application a form used to record information regarding a credit applicant's ability to repay the debt.

Credit bureau an agency which gathers credit information about customers.

Credit limit a specified amount beyond which a credit customer may not buy on credit.

Credit memorandum a form issued by a seller to a buyer indicating that the seller is reducing the amount the buyer owes.

Credit rating a rating to help the business determine if a credit applicant should be granted credit. It is based on factors such as the applicant's job history, income, assets owned, and credit history.

Credit receipt written evidence of merchandise returned and the selling price.

Debit memorandum a form issued by a seller to a buyer indicating that the seller is increasing the amount the buyer owes.

Deductible the amount that an insured must pay on any insured loss before payment by the insurance company begins.

Default failure to meet the conditions of a loan contract. It generally refers to the failure to meet interest and/or principal payments.

Discharge of bankruptcy an order in which the bankrupt debtor is relieved of responsibility to pay his or her obligations.

157

Discount loan a loan in which the whole interest charge is deducted in advance from the face value of a loan reducing the proceeds received. This increases the effective interest cost of the loan.

Diversification the spreading of risk such as by carrying different product lines.

Dunning letter notices that insistently demand repayment of debts from customers.

Effective date the day a contract begins. After the effective date of the agreement, the parties are bound by it.

Effective interest rate real rate of interest on a loan. It is the nominal interest divided by the loan proceeds.

Employment contract a legal agreement between the employer and employee specifying the particulars of the arrangement, such as employment terms and compensation.

Entrepreneurial profit the net income earned by the hard-working owner of a business.

Equal credit opportunity act a federal law making it illegal to discriminate when giving credit.

Exchange a customer returns merchandise and obtains merchandise of equal value in return.

Express warranty a manufacturer's voluntary written warranty that accompanies its product.

Extended coverage protection over and above that given by an insurance policy.

Extended warranty a service contract providing protection over and above that given by the warranty available with a new product.

Financial leverage the ratio of debt to equity.

Fixed cost a cost that remains the same each period in the short run regardless of activity. Examples are rent, insurance, and property taxes.

Flexible budget an estimate of income and costs based on different projections of sales volume.

Full warranty a type of warranty that entitles consumers to full remedies for defective goods or services for a specified period of time.

General partner a partner who has unlimited liability for partnership debts in the event the partnership fails. The general partner manages the business.

Gift certificate a certificate generally paid for by one person and entitling the recipient to obtain merchandise, food, or services at no charge up to the amount paid by the purchaser.

Gross profit margin ratio of gross profit to net sales. A high gross profit margin is a positive sign since it shows the business is earning an attractive return over the cost of its merchandise sold.

Illiquid 1. Lacking enough liquid assets, like cash and marketable securities, to cover short-term obligations. 2. Current liabilities exceed current assets.

Impaired credit a reduction in credit given by a business to a customer who has experienced a deterioration in creditworthiness.

Implied warranty a warranty in effect whether expressed individually or not. It is mandated by state law. It provides the products sold are warranted to be suitable for sale and will work effectively whether there is an express warranty or not.

Installment credit a type of consumer credit in which the consumer pays the amount owed in equal payments, usually monthly.

Installment loan a loan that is repaid in a series of periodic, fixed scheduled payments instead of in a lump sum.

Installment sale a sale in which periodic cash payments will be received over time.

Ironclad contract a legal contract that will be very difficult to break.

Keogh pension plan a tax-deferred retirement plan under which self-employed persons have the right to establish retirement plans for themselves and their employers. The contributions are tax deductible, and earnings are tax deferred until withdrawn. Self-employed individuals can contribute to their Keogh plan up to 25 percent of earnings, or a maximum of $30,000.

Lease a contract in which the lessee pays rent to the

lessor in order to use real property for a designated time period.

Leverage the use of borrowed money to magnify potential returns from the business. It is hoped that the investment through leverage will earn a rate of return greater than the after-tax costs of borrowing.

License a legal document given by a regulatory agency to a business to conduct some activity subject to prescribed terms. Typically, a fee is charged. An example is a liquor license.

Lien a claim of a party, typically a creditor, to hold or control the property of another party to satisfy a debt. It permits the creditor to liquidate the property that serves as collateral in the event of default.

Limited partner a member of a partnership whose liability for the debts of the partnership is limited to the member's investment. A limited partner is not allowed to take active part in the management of a partnership.

Line of credit the maximum preapproved amount that a business may borrow.

Liquid the state of having sufficient cash and near-cash assets to meet current debt.

List price the standard published price of a good or service.

Markdown a reduction in the original retail selling price.

Markup 1. An increase in the original selling price. 2. Adding a profit to cost to determine a selling price.

Mechanic's lien a lien placed against property by an unpaid service business in which the owner can hold on to the property until the customer pays for services rendered.

Negative cash flow a situation in which cash inflows are less than cash outflows. This is an unfavorable situation that may result in liquidity problems.

Net worth total assets less total liabilities. This represents the owner's equity in the business.

Offer 1. A proposal to perform some activity or to pay some money. Once an offer is accepted, a contract exists. 2. To offer a good or service for sale.

Open account 1. An account having a balance, such as

one in which a customer still owes the retail store money. 2. A credit relationship between seller and buyer.

Payback period the number of years it takes to recover your initial investment. The payback period equals the initial investment divided by the annual cash inflow.

Payment plan a plan specifying the dates and amounts of payments to be made under a financing agreement.

Payroll withholding the amount taken out of an employee's salary for taxes and other items (e.g., union dues) to be remitted to other parties (e.g., IRS).

Professional liability insurance an insurance policy taken out by a professional for malpractice coverage. The policy covers legal fees and possible damages.

Profit margin ratio of net income to net sales. It reveals the entity's ability to generate profit at a given sales level. The ratio gives the owner an indicator of the operating efficiency and pricing strategy of the business.

Recourse a business owner's right to recover from a customer payment for something sold or services performed.

Refund amount paid back or credit given because of the return of merchandise.

Return the reward for investing in a business in the form of earnings and appreciation in the value of the business.

Risk 1. Variability about income, returns, or other financial variable. 2. Possibility of losing value.

Risk adverse opposed to risk. It is a subjective attitude against risk taking.

Risk management the analysis of and planning for potential risk and their subsequent losses. The objective of risk management is to try to minimize the financial consequence of random losses.

Risk reduction an attempt by a business owner to minimize risk by taking some action such as diversifying and obtaining insurance coverage.

Risk-return trade-off a comparison of the expected return from an investment with the risk associated with it. The higher the risk undertaken, the more ample the return. Conversely, the lower the risk, the more modest the return.

Sales contract an agreement between the seller and buyer specifying the terms of sale.

Sales tax a state or local tax based on a percentage of the selling price of a good or service that the buyer pays. The seller collects the tax and remits it to the sales tax agency.

Seasonality a fluctuation in business conditions that occur on a regular basis. It may be caused by such factors as weather and vacations. An example is the toy industry, which has its greatest sales in November and December.

Secured loan a loan requiring certain assets to be pledged as collateral.

Self-employed income the net taxable income of a self-employed person reported on Schedule C of IRS Form 1040. The self-employed individual pays a higher social security tax than a regular employee.

Service contract an agreement in which the seller or other third party will repair merchandise purchased by a buyer.

Simple interest the interest charge computed on the original principal.

Term loan intermediate to long-term secured loan granted to a business by a commercial bank, insurance company, or commercial finance company usually to finance capital equipment or provide working capital. The loan is amortized over a fixed period.

Tight money a situation in which fewer funds are made available to borrowers by lending institutions and creditors. If available, the loans carry higher interest rates.

Time value of money value of money at different time periods. In other words, $1 today is worth more than $1 tomorrow. The time of money is a critical consideration in financial decisions.

Title the legal right of an ownership interest in a property. It is evidence of ownership and lawful possession.

Total return the return received over a specified time period from periodic income and capital gain on sale.

Trade association an organization representing the interests of businesses in the same industry.

Truth in lending act a federal law protecting credit purchases. The most important provision is the requirement that both the dollar amount of finance charges and the annual percentage rate charged be disclosed.

Turnover the number of times an asset, such as inventory, turns over during an accounting period.

Underinsurance the failure to carry sufficient insurance.

Unlimited liability amount of risk borne by someone in a sole proprietorship or general partnership. Liability is not restricted to the capital investments, thus, if the business goes bankrupt, the owner risks his or her personal assets to meet creditor claims. In a corporation, however, the stockholder has limited liability up to his/her investment.

Unsecured loan a loan on which no collateral is required.

INDEX